APPLICATIONS OF CASE STUDY RESEARCH

Robert K. Yin

Applied Social Research Methods Series
Volume 34

13704

SAGE Publications
International Educational and Professional Publisher
Newbury Park   London   New Delhi

To Karen

For information address:

SAGE Publications, Inc.
2455 Teller Road
Newbury Park, California 91320

SAGE Publications Ltd.
6 Bonhill Street
London EC2A 4PU
United Kingdom

SAGE Publications India Pvt. Ltd.
M-32 Market
Greater Kailash I
New Delhi 110 048 India

Printed in the United States of America

Library of Congress Cataloging-in-Publication Data

Yin, Robert K.
   Applications of case study research / Robert K. Yin.
       p.   cm.—(Applied social research methods series; v. 34)
   Includes bibliographical references and indexes.
   ISBN 0-8039-5118-3 (cloth). —ISBN 0-8039-5119-1 (pbk.)
   1. Social sciences—Methodology. 2. Case method. I. Title.
II. Series.
H61.Y56   1993
300'.722—dc20   93-14934

   94 95 96 10 9 8 7 6 5 4 3 2

Sage Production Editor: Tara S. Mead

97

This book is due for return on or before the last date shown below.

Applied Social Research Methods Series
Volume 34

Contents

Preface and Acknowledgments

Almost 10 years have passed since the initial publication and eight printings of the first edition of *Case Study Research: Design and Methods* (Yin, 1984/1989). That earlier textbook has served as possibly the only primer for using case studies as a research tool. The intervening years have seen continued interest—even growth—in this use of case studies. The earlier text itself has subsequently had a revised edition, with more than 13 additional printings to date.

This book, *Applications of Case Study Research,* is intended to augment the earlier work by providing students and research investigators with extensive applications of actual case study research and with discussions of how case study research can be applied to broad areas of inquiry. Nearly all the examples come from projects carried out at COSMOS Corporation, an independent, applied social science research think tank. At COSMOS, this kind of research continues to this day, and the staff at COSMOS—especially Peter Bateman—deserve much of the credit for assisting in the conduct of this case study research.

In addition, by way of acknowledgment, the work in this book reflects the stimulation and continued encouragement and support of many persons. The editors of this Sage Publications' series on Applied Social Research Methods—Professor Leonard Bickman and Dr. Debra Rog—have been strong supporters from the very beginning. They are to be thanked for their understanding of the place of case study research in the broader array of social science methods and for their incessant demands for better manuscripts on the topic. Discussions at semiannual meetings with Michael Bailin (President) and his staff, when I served as a member of the research advisory board for Public/Private Ventures, Inc., also were highly instrumental in forcing the explicit description of specific methodological procedures to solve ongoing research problems.

As usual, students and faculty colleagues also have stimulated the development of new ideas. These include continued questions posed about the case study method by students enrolled in the Advanced Technology Management Program at the American University in the fall of 1986—and in subsequent courses on the case study method at that university's School of International Service (1987 and 1988)—and those enrolled in Ph.D.

programs in Denmark and Scandinavia who attended the Sandbjerg summer institutes (1989 and 1991) sponsored by the Aarhus School of Business (University of Aarhus) in Denmark. Faculty who helped put these courses into the curriculum and who then invited me to teach them include Associate Dean Nanette S. Levinson of the School of International Service and Professors Erik Albaek, Finn Borum, and Erik Maaloe of the Aarhus School of Business.

Expressions of interest and inquiry from those using the method in different fields and places over the years also have served as a stimulating source and include the following: Professor Allen Lee, Northeastern University, who organized a session on the case study method at the 1986 annual meeting of the Society of Management; Professor Rod White, University of Western Ontario, who similarly organized a seminar on qualitative methods at the university's business school; Marianne C. H. Donker, The Netherlands Institute of Mental Health, who organized its first National Congress on Evaluation in 1991; Jo Kloprogge, Institute for Educational Research in the Netherlands; and Willem van der Eyken, Bernard van Leer Foundation of the Netherlands.

Versions of four of the six chapters in this book were first solicited to appear as articles in separate journals or books.

- A shorter version of Chapter 1 appeared in Huey T. Chen and Peter H. Rossi (Eds.), *Theory-Driven Evaluation in Analyzing Policies and Programs* (Westport, CT: Greenwood Press, 1992), pp. 97-114.
- A shorter version of Chapter 2 appeared in Marvin Alkin (Ed.), *Encyclopedia of Educational Research,* 6th ed. (New York: Macmillan, 1992).
- A shorter version of Chapter 3 appeared in James I. Cash and Paul R. Lawrence (Eds.), *The Information Systems Research Challenge: Qualitative Research Methods* (Boston, MA: Harvard Business School, 1989), pp. 1-6.
- A shorter version of Chapter 4 first appeared in *Current Sociology, 40*(Spring 1992), 121-137.

In addition, abbreviated versions of Chapters 5 and 6 were presented at workshops in 1991, held in Washington, DC.

I therefore owe a large measure of thanks to the editors who initially solicited the four papers that now appear as chapters in this book—Professor Huey Chen (Akron University), Professor Marvin Alkin (UCLA), Professors James Cash and Paul Lawrence (Harvard Business School), and Professor Jacques Hamel (University of Montreal). All of these editors pressed me to create and complete the needed manuscripts—and to do so in a timely manner. The manuscripts benefited also from anonymous peer reviewers and obsessive copy editors. Chapter 3 also was the result of a most stimulating seminar at the Harvard Business School organized by Professors Cash and Lawrence and therefore benefited from the other participants at the seminar, especially Professor John Van Maanen, MIT, and Professor Lynne M. Markus, UCLA. Similarly, the participants at the workshop for the paper that later became Chapter 5 helped clarify the ideas presented in that paper and included Alan Ginsburg, Director, Planning and Evaluation Service, U.S. Department of Education; Professor Richard Light, Harvard University; Professor Donald Campbell, Lehigh University; and Professor Robert Boruch, University of Pennsylvania.

Finally, I would like to dedicate this book to Karen, my lover, spouse, friend, and mother of our son, Andrew Lukas. She has continually nurtured great expectations for both of us, and her love has endured the many hours absorbed by the writing, travel, and presentations associated with the ideas in this book.

Introduction

Case study research continues to be an essential form of social science inquiry. The method is appropriate when investigators desire to (a) define topics broadly and not narrowly, (b) cover contextual conditions and not just the phenomenon of study, and (c) rely on multiple and not singular sources of evidence. The method should be part of a social scientist's complete armamentarium, which also should include the use of surveys, the conduct of experiments, the analyses of archival (quantitative) records, and historiography. Thus depending on the circumstance, a social scientist needs to be able to apply any of these five methods, sometimes even in combination with each other.

A desire for increased methodological guidance on how to carry out case study research has accompanied the continued use of the method. As an example, the author alone has encountered numerous groups of researchers and students seeking assistance. Their research has covered such diverse topics as business and organizational issues, education, child development and youth policy, family studies, international affairs, evaluation, technology development, and research on social problems. Unfortunately, existing modes of information dissemination do not adequately provide the forums either to develop or to convey such guidance. For instance, no journal of case studies exists and no journal focuses exclusively on case study methods. Similarly, the most common textbooks on social science in general (e.g., Kidder, Judd, & Smith, 1986) or on evaluation research methods (e.g., Rossi & Freeman, 1993) hardly mention case studies. Not surprisingly, lessons about case study research have cumulated slowly and rather inefficiently.

The purpose of *Applications of Case Study Research* is therefore to review key aspects of the case study method by presenting multiple and in-depth applications from actual research. None of the applications is a complete case study. Instead, each application illustrates one or more principles described in an earlier text (Yin, 1984/1989). All of the applications come from longer, completed investigations by the author, which have been referenced in the text for further inquiry. The main goal of the applications is to help students and researchers identify solutions to problems encountered when doing case study research. These solutions can be used again, or they may suggest yet other solutions that will meet a specific need.

APPLICATIONS OR ADVANCES?

In assembling these applications, an interesting question arises: Do they merely represent applications of case study research, or might they also reflect consistent methodological *advances* in the state of the art of case study research? The argument for advances would be that the applications include some new methodological concepts and procedures as well as more attention to those that only received minor attention in the earlier text (Yin, 1984/1989). Such concepts and procedures include the following.

- Special attention to case selection and screening (see Chapter 1)
- An example of the need for theory in conducting descriptive, and not just causal, case studies (see Chapter 1)
- Comparisons between the case study method and four related methods— grounded theory, ethnography, quasi-experimentation, and experimentation (see Chapters 3 and 4)
- The case study as an evaluation tool (see Chapters 4 and 5)
- The case study as a conceptual umbrella for multiple substudies (see Chapter 6)

In the final analysis, even though some new or previously less popularized concepts and procedures appear in this book, the notion of "advances" was discarded. To claim an advance requires more than the presentation of a new concept or procedure. One must also show that the new practice (concept or procedure) is better than the previously used practice. The examples in this book are not intended to provide such evidence, nor are there any explicit comparisons to demonstrate such advances.

However, you should know that methodological advances in the case study method are still desired. The major contribution of the earlier text (Yin, 1984/1989) was to formalize and document an ongoing craft. At this time, the case study craft can benefit enormously from methodological advances. The most important advances to be sought are those that would help make case studies be less cumbersome to do; be easier to read and disseminate; and, above all, be of higher quality and have data more readily disentangled from interpretation. Consistent methodological demonstrations of this sort would deserve to be accompanied by a book title such as *Advances in Case Study Research*. The examples in this book are possibly a step in this direction, but they do not fall within the comparative framework needed to warrant this alternative title.

TOPICS COVERED AND
THE ORGANIZATION OF THIS BOOK

The presentation of examples of specific applications of case study research nevertheless serves an unfilled need. Reviews of the earlier text on case study research (Yin, 1984/1989) commonly congratulated it for its well-organized presentation of procedures but also criticized it for not showing, in depth, how case study research could actually be carried out. The applications in the present book are cumulatively intended to respond to these reviews and to the continued needs expressed by researchers and students. To facilitate the use of the book, Table A.1 cross-references the various methodological and substantive topics covered by each chapter in this book. The table shows that the selected examples cover a wide range of substantive topics, and that they also place the case study method in a comparative framework of available social science methods. Such a comparative framework is intended to help investigators know when the case study method might be preferable over other methods (and when it might not).

This book is organized into three parts. Part I contains a single, comprehensive chapter (Chapter 1) on the role of theory in doing case studies. This single topic is possibly the most critical component in case study research. *Theory* not only is helpful in designing a case study, but it also later becomes the vehicle for generalizing a case study's results. This critical role of theory has been integral to the development of sound case studies—whether consisting of single or multiple cases. Part I therefore shows how to integrate theoretical concerns into exploratory case studies, descriptive case studies, and causal case studies. Part I also shows how theory can even enter the picture during the case selection process. You should know that, if no other lesson is learned from this book, an understanding of the use of theory and an appreciation for the examples in Part I will go a long way toward designing implementable, useful, and generalizable case studies.

Part II contains two chapters. Each focuses on case study design issues in a policy topic frequently investigated by using case studies: education (Chapter 2) and management information systems (Chapter 3). The two chapters provide simple reminders and cautions when doing design, including further illustrations of the importance of theory. These chapters contain multiple examples from education and management information systems, providing examples of such important steps as selecting the units

Table A.1

Subjects Covered by Chapters in This Book

Subject	Chapter					
	1	*2*	*3*	*4*	*5*	*6*
Topical:						
Community-Based Interventions						■
Computer Software Development			■			
Education		■				
Gangs				■		
High-Risk Youth					■	■
High-Tech Parks	■					
Innovation	■					
Job Training	■					
Local Economic Development	■					
Management Information Systems			■			
Partnerships	■	■				
Research Utilization	■					
Students With Disabilities	■					
Substance Abuse					■	■
Methodological:						
Demonstrations				■	■	■
Ethnography			■	■		
Evaluation				■	■	■
Experiments					■	
Grounded Theory				■		
Quasi-Experiments					■	■

of analysis, defining the data collection needs (a design step), and establishing rival hypotheses.

Part III introduces an entirely different theme—the use of case studies as an evaluation tool. This use of the case study method in doing evaluations has not been given much attention, even though such applications have become increasingly popular. The purpose of this final part of the book is therefore to expose you to the full range of evaluation issues and to how methodological barriers can be overcome, including these topics: distinctions among different qualitative research strategies (Chapter 4); case study designs focusing on different units of analyses in evaluations (Chapter 5); and the application of the case study logic to the evaluation of highly complex interventions, such as community-based interventions (Chapter 6). These three chapters are intended also to suggest possibilities

Table A.2

List of "Boxed" Vignettes

for advancing the state of the art in using case studies for evaluation. For this reason, the final chapter ("Summing Up") actually concludes by noting that complex evaluations may have to consist of multiple substudies; but the overall evaluation itself may be construed as a case study, with the multiple substudies being embedded units of analysis.

Overall, the three parts of this book provide you with numerous, specific, and workable applications of case study research. The major emphasis is on theory and design. As with the earlier text, less attention has been given to topics on data collection and fieldwork—topics that continue to be covered well by other texts.

To guide you further, strewn throughout the book is a series of "boxed" vignettes. Each vignette covers a key methodological concept or term, so that you can more readily "apprentice" with the text. For easy reference, Table A.2 lists the 17 boxes and their topics, along with the page numbers on which the boxes will be found.

In addition, as with other texts in this series, a brief set of exercises appears at the end of each chapter. These exercises are intended to stimulate your further thinking on key topics.

ON EMULATING THE SCIENTIFIC METHOD

Readers familiar with the earlier text will know that its approach to case study research favors the emulation of the scientific method. The steps in this method commonly include the following: the posing of clear questions and the development of a formal research design; the use of theory and reviews of previous research to develop hypotheses and rival hypotheses; the collection of empirical data to test these hypotheses and rival hypotheses; the assembling of a database—independent of any narrative report, interpretations, or conclusions—that can be inspected by third parties; and the conduct of quantitative or qualitative analyses (or both), depending on the topic and research design.

This book continues the emulation of the scientific method. Such a method is considered an essential way of improving the quality of case study research. However, because emulation has been espoused as a desirable goal, some critics of this approach to case studies have mistaken such emulation as a claim that doing case studies in this manner is the same as doing science. You should know that no one yet has the evidence or argument to make this claim. My only claim is that case studies that follow procedures from "normal" science are likely to be of higher quality than case studies that do not. But doing case studies is not necessarily the same as doing science (just as doing social science is not necessarily the same as doing natural science), and the matter deserves clarification. I hope that readers will share in the clarification process.

PART I

Theory

1

The Role of Theory in Doing Case Studies

WHAT IS THE CASE STUDY METHOD?

The case study is the method of choice when the phenomenon under study is not readily distinguishable from its context. Such a phenomenon may be a *project* or *program* in an evaluation study. Sometimes the definition of this project or program may be problematic, as in determining when the activity started or ended—an example of a complex interaction between a phenomenon and its (temporal) context. Other examples of such complex interactions abound—covering such varied situations as microcomputer implementation (Yin & White, 1985), urban high schools (Yin & White, 1986), advanced technologies (Yin & Moore, 1987), community organizations (Yin et al., 1987), interorganizational partnerships (Yin et al., 1989), and management information systems (see Chapter 3). These are typical situations warranting the use of case studies.

The inclusion of the context as a major part of a study, however, creates distinctive technical challenges. First, the richness of the context means that the ensuing study will likely have more variables than data points. Second, the richness means that the study cannot rely on a single data collection method but will likely need to use multiple sources of evidence. Third, even if all the relevant variables are quantitative, distinctive strategies will be needed for research design and for analysis. The development of rigorous techniques and strategies under these conditions—in comparison to the conditions faced by ethnography, history, quasi-experimentation, and surveys—has been the continuing quest in defining the case study method (see Chapters 4 and 5). Further, a continuing priority is to consider case studies as a method not implying any particular form of data collection—which can be quantitative or qualitative (Yin, 1984/1989).

AUTHOR'S NOTE: This chapter is an expanded and adapted version of a paper appearing in Huey T. Chen and Peter H. Rossi (Eds.), *Theory-Driven Evaluation in Analyzing Policies and Programs* (pp. 97-114, 1992). An imprint of Greenwood Publishing Group, Inc., Westport, CT. Used with permission.

WHAT IS THE ROLE OF THEORY
IN DOING CASE STUDIES?

Among the strategies has been the explicit role of theory in establishing expectations for analyzing a case study's empirical evidence. Not surprisingly, revived interest in the role of theory in doing evaluations (Bickman, 1987; Chen, 1990; Chen & Rossi, 1989) has had a continued counterpart in the design of case studies. Critical examples include the importance of theory in explanatory, and not just exploratory or descriptive, case studies (Yin, 1981a) as well as in multiple-case studies based on replication designs (Yin, 1981b). Overall, theory can be important to case studies in many ways, helping to do the following.

- Select the cases to be studied in the first place, whether following a single-case or multiple-case (replication) design (see Box 1)
- Specify what is being explored when you are doing exploratory case studies
- Define a complete and appropriate description when you are doing descriptive case studies
- Stipulate rival theories when you are doing explanatory case studies (also see Box 1)
- Generalize the results to other cases

From this perspective, the term *theory* covers more than causal theories. Rather, *theory* means the design of research steps according to some relationship to the literature, policy issues, or other substantive source. Excluded would be considerations of access, convenience, logistics, or nonsubstantive issues. Good use of theory will help delimit a case study inquiry to its most effective design; theory is also essential for generalizing the subsequent results.

The purpose of this chapter is to provide specific illustrations of theory-based approaches to case study research and evaluations. Many of the classic illustrations have been cited elsewhere (Yin, 1984/1989; also see Chapters 2 and 3 of this book). Therefore, the examples in the present chapter all come from the author's own research experience. Reported below are applications of theory in exploratory case studies, case study selection, two types of causal case studies, and descriptive case studies.

EXPLORATORY CASE STUDIES

The exploratory case study has perhaps given all of case study research its most notorious reputation. In this type of case study, fieldwork and

---

BOX 1
Six Different Types of Case Studies

Case study research can be based on *single-* or *multiple-*case studies. Further—whether single or multiple—the case study can be *exploratory, descriptive,* or *explanatory.* Thus your own case study may potentially fall into at least six (2 × 3) basic types of case studies, disregarding differences in design within each type.

In a nutshell, the 2 × 3 dimensions may be characterized as follows (see Yin, 1984/1989 for more details). A single-case study focuses on a single case only. Multiple-case studies, however, include two or more cases within the same study. These multiple cases should be selected so that they are replicating each other—either exact (direct) replications or predictably different (systematic) replications.

An exploratory case study (whether based on single or multiple cases) is aimed at defining the questions and hypotheses of a subsequent (not necessarily case) study or at determining the feasibility of the desired research procedures. A descriptive case study presents a complete description of a phenomenon within its context. An explanatory case study presents data bearing on cause-effect relationships—explaining which causes produced which effects.

---

data collection are undertaken prior to the final definition of study questions and hypotheses. Research may follow intuitive paths, perceived by others as sloppy. However, you may be genuinely trying to discover theory by directly observing a social phenomenon in its "raw" form (Glaser & Strauss, 1967). Moreover, when the final study questions and hypotheses are settled, your final study may not necessarily be a case study but may assume some other form. The exploratory case study (see Box 2), therefore, has been considered a prelude to much social research, not just to other case studies (e.g., Ogawa & Malen, 1991; Yin, 1991).

An illustrative use of the exploratory case study occurred as part of a study on how innovations in urban services become "routinized" (Yin, 1981c; Yin, 1982; Yin et al., 1979). Service agencies were experiencing difficulties in making such innovations survive beyond the adoption phase. This meant that an innovation might be put into place for a 2- or 3-year period, show promising results, but then stop being used. The policy relevance of the study was to determine how to avoid such an outcome.

The exploratory case studies were conducted during the pilot-test phase of the fuller study, which involved 12 case studies and a telephone survey of 90 other sites. The study team spent an extended time in the exploratory

---

BOX 2
Exploratory Case Studies

Possibly the major problem with exploratory case studies is that the data collected during the pilot phase are then also used as part of any ensuing case study. Whether a case study involves single or multiple cases, you should not permit such slippage from the exploratory (or pilot) phase into the actual case study to occur.

You should take an exploratory study at its face value. Your investigator may have initially been uncertain about some major aspect of a "real" study—the questions to be asked, the hypotheses of study, the data collection methods, the access to the data, or the data analytic methods—and therefore needed to investigate these issues. Once investigated, the pilot or exploratory phase should be considered completed. Now, you are ready to start the "real" study—with a complete research design, a whole new set of sources (sites) of information, and a fresh set of data—from scratch.

Further, the pilot study might have pointed to the need for a survey, experiment, or some method different from a case study. The exploratory case study was still a case study and might have yielded invaluable results; however, the ensuing "real" study still needs to be conducted.

---

phase and collected substantial data from 7 sites (none of which was used in the final study). Such a high proportion of pilot to final case study sites (7 to 12) is exceptional, but the study team had major questions in need of answers.

The Exploratory Issue: The Need to Create a Framework of Study. Only the broad features of the study design had been determined ahead of time. First, the study team was to select different types of innovations, covering different urban services. Second, the team would follow a retrospective design: The sites to be studied would be ones where the routinization of an innovation was known to have occurred, so that the entire routinization process could be studied, even though the data had to be collected retrospectively. Third, the study team would emphasize actual behavioral events in the routinization processes, in contrast to an alternative methodology focusing on people's perceptions. However, within these broader themes, the specific design and data collection methods were unspecified. Thus a pilot phase was designed to determine the innovations and services to be studied as well as the conceptual framework and operational measures to be used.

A key ingredient here was the use of a special pilot protocol, which elaborated alternative features about the "life cycle" of an innovation. The study team understood that adoption-implementation-routinization potentially constituted the entire life cycle but had not developed specific hypotheses or measures to facilitate empirical study. In this sense, the protocol reflected the development of theory, not just methodological issues. The study team modified this protocol after every pilot site study was completed. This iterative process forced the team to ask itself these questions repeatedly: Had sufficient information been learned that an existing exploratory question could now be dropped? Had new problems emerged, requiring the framing of a new question? Had an existing question needed to be modified? The pilot testing evolved in the following fashion. The first site visit covered five different innovations, but not in much depth. Later site visits narrowed to one or two innovations, but with increasing data collection about each one. Ultimately, hypotheses and the instrumentation for a full profile of an innovation's life history emerged.

Illustrative Results and Key Lessons. The pilot testing helped to identify six innovations in three urban services (police, education, and fire) that were ultimately studied at over 100 sites. However, the most important result of the pilot testing was the development of a conceptual framework and operational measures of a hypothesized routinization process. Measurable organizational events were identified as "cycles" or "passages," as illustrated in Table 1.1. Further, certain cycles and passages were predicted to occur earlier in the routinization process and others later. The framework made it possible for data to be collected and the full study to proceed.

Another important result of the pilot testing was the finding that whereas a single protocol could be used for the case studies, the study team had to design six separate questionnaires for the telephone survey— one for each type of innovation. For phone interviews, the terminology and events were sufficiently different that a generic set of questions could not be used. Such a discovery meant much unanticipated work on the part of the study team, and in fact the finding was resisted throughout the pilot phase because of the known consequences in work load. However, no single questionnaire would work.

This experience with pilot testing shows how explicit explorations can elaborate key conceptual topics within some previously identified, broad subject area. The use of a pilot protocol is strongly suggested as a tool for assuring that the exploration is following some exploratory "theory," and that you are not merely wandering through the exploratory phase.

Table 1.1

Organizational Passages and Cycles Related to Routinization

Type of Resource or Operation	Passages	Cycles
Budget	Innovation supports changes from soft to hard money	Survives annual budget cycles
Personnel:		
Jobs	Functions become part of job descriptions or prerequisites	—
Incumbent turnover	—	Survives introduction of new personnel Survives promotion of key personnel
Training:		
Prepractice	Skills become part of professional standards, professional school curriculum	—
Inservice	—	Skills taught during many training cycles
Organizational governance	Innovative activity attains appropriate organizational status Use of innovation becomes part of statute, regulation, manual, and so on	Attains widespread use
Supply and maintenance	Supply and maintenance is provided by agency or on long-term (contract) basis	Survives equipment turnover

Source: Yin, 1981c.

CASE SELECTION AND SCREENING CRITERIA AND PROCEDURES

Selecting the case or cases to be studied is one of the most difficult steps in case study research. When you are uncertain of this process, the elaboration of theoretical issues—related to the objectives of study—can provide essential guidance.

The Research Issue: Linking Job Training and Economic Development at the Local Level. An illustration of the difficulties of this process, and how they were overcome, is a study of local job training and economic development efforts (Yin et al., 1989). The example illustrates an extended selection process, to help you develop a full appreciation of the potential steps. Many studies may not need to use all of these steps or undertake them in such detail. However, the example provides a comprehensive template.

The study objective was to investigate how linkages between job training (for the hard-to-employ) and economic development efforts can produce distinctive outcomes. The potential advantages are that, for the training participant, placement is more likely to occur in jobs in growing industries and growing occupations, resulting in more enduring job placements. Conversely, for employers, a larger pool of appropriately trained employees is created, thereby making recruitment easier. Without such linkages between job training and economic development, neither advantage is likely to be realized. Job training efforts alone can easily lead to placement in low-growth jobs for the hard-to-employ; economic development efforts alone can focus too heavily on employers' facilities and capital needs and overlook their potential employment needs.

A series of case studies was to examine these linkage situations and how these outcomes were produced. However, although linkage was simple in concept, it was difficult to define operationally. What kinds of cases would be relevant?

Unit of Analysis. One challenge was to define the unit of analysis (see Box 3). The study team readily understood that this unit would not necessarily be a single organization or initiative. For linkage, a joint organizational effort (between two or more organizations) or joint initiatives (job training and economic development) would likely be the unit of analysis. The identification of such joint efforts therefore became the first characteristic of the unit of analysis.

A further and more troubling characteristic involved the context for such joint efforts. At the local level, such efforts can occur in at least three different contexts: a joint project, a joint program, or an interorganizational effort. Joint projects included such examples as a community college offering a class, in conjunction with an employer in a high-growth industry, focusing on the employer's job openings. The study team found numerous examples of these joint projects in the published literature. Among joint programs were such examples as a statewide dislocated worker program, to provide training to dislocated workers. In general, these programmatic efforts were more sustained than single projects. In addition, in the previous few years, many states in the country had taken such initiatives.

In contrast, the interorganizational context did not focus on a single project or program. Rather, the qualifying criterion was that two or more organizations had joined in some arrangement—by forming a joint venture, initiating a consortium, or using interagency agreements among existing organizations—to conduct training and economic development activities together.

BOX 3
The Unit of Analysis—A Critical Concept
in Doing Case Studies

No issue is more important than defining the unit of analysis. "What is my case?" is the question most frequently posed by those doing case studies. Without a tentative answer, you will not know how to limit the boundaries of your study. Because case studies permit you to collect data from many perspectives—and for time periods of undetermined duration—you must clearly define the unit of analysis at the outset of your study. The unit of analysis has another critical significance in doing case studies. The findings of the case study will pertain to specific theoretical propositions about the defined unit of analysis. These propositions will later be the means for generalizing the findings of the case study—to similar cases focusing on the same unit of analysis. Thus the entire design of the case study as well as its potential theoretical significance is heavily dominated by the way the unit of analysis is defined.

With regard to these three contexts, theory and policy relevance played the critical role in the study team's final choice. First, the existing literature indicated that the three contexts were different—cases of one were not to be confused with cases of the others. For instance, programs call for more significant outlays than projects, and interorganizational arrangements may be the most troublesome but can then be the occasion for multiple programs and projects.

Second, the literature had given less attention to interorganizational arrangements, even though they had more promise of local capacity-building in the long run. Thus a local area with a workable interorganizational arrangement may sustain many efforts and may not be as vulnerable to the sporadic nature of single projects or programs.

Third, the study team was interested in advancing knowledge about interorganizational arrangements. In the 1980s, considerable public effort had been made to create "public-private" partnerships, not just in employment and economic development but also in many services for disadvantaged population groups—housing, education, social services, health and mental health care, and community development. Such interests have continued into the 1990s. Yet, the available literature was (and still is) shallow with regard to the workings of interorganizational arrangements—how they are formed, what makes them thrive, and how to sustain them.

Finally, a study of interorganizational arrangements could also include coverage of component programs or projects—within the arrangements—

as embedded units of analysis. In this way, the study could still touch on all three contexts. For all these reasons, the study team selected the interorganizational arrangement as the unit of analysis to be studied.

Criteria for Selecting Cases. The selection of multiple cases was part of the initial design. However, one constraint was that only a small number of cases could be the subject of study, because the study team wanted to collect data extensively from each interorganizational arrangement—collecting data directly from each of the participating organizations rather than merely surveying the "lead" organization. This constraint was again based on theoretical issues, because of the study team's desire to investigate the dynamics of each arrangement and not just to apply some input-output framework. The team also suspected that no single organization would have accurate information on what might turn out to be a diversity of programs and projects within each arrangement.

A further constraint was the study's need to inform national policy. Although no representational sampling scheme could be used with such a small number of cases, some distributive factors still demanded attention. Overall, multiple cases were required, but only a small number could be studied, leading to the use of a replication logic for selecting the final cases.

In using the replication logic, the first selection criterion was that every case had to demonstrate—prior to final case selection—the occurrence of exemplary outcomes. This exemplary case design has been cited as an important use of case studies (Ginsburg, 1989)—see Box 4. The basic replication question would then be whether similar events within each arrangement could account for these outcomes. A second criterion reflected the study's policy concern—some of the arrangements would have a federally supported type of organization at its center, but other arrangements would have it in a more peripheral relationship. A third criterion was that the cases would cover different regions of the country, emphasizing different economic conditions—reflected in the stereotypic notions of "sunbelt," "snowbelt," and "rustbelt."

As a result of these considerations, the study team sought six cases. All had to have documented and exemplary outcomes that could survive the study team's screening procedures. Three of the cases would have a key, federally supported organization at each one's center; the other three would have such an organization in a more peripheral relationship. Together, the six cases would have to cover some distribution of different geographic and economic conditions.

BOX 4
Exemplary Case Designs

The specific cases to be studied may be selected by following several different rationales, one of which is to select "exemplary" cases. Use of this rationale means that all of the cases will reflect strong, positive examples of the phenomenon of interest. The rationale fits a replication logic (see Box 7) well, because your overall investigation may then try to determine whether similar causal events—within each case—produced these positive outcomes.

The use of the exemplary case design, however, also requires you to determine—beforehand—if specific cases indeed have produced exemplary outcomes. Extensive case screening may be needed, and you must resist permitting the case screening process to become a study in itself.

Case Screening. The final selection criteria led to a major effort for screening candidate cases. Such an effort is not an unusual adjunct of using the replication logic, and you must plan for sufficient time and resources to support the screening process. A pitfall to be avoided is to allow the screening to be so extensive that, in fact, "mini" case studies are done as part of the screening. However, you must be prepared to collect and analyze actual empirical data at this stage.

The study team began this screening process by contacting numerous individuals in the field and consulting available reports and literature. These sources were used to suggest candidates that fit the selection criteria, resulting in a list of 62 nominees. The study team then attempted to contact these nominees, both by writing and by phone. The team obtained information on 47 of them.

The information was based on responses to a structured interview of about 45 minutes—using a formal instrument. Each of the candidate arrangements also was encouraged to submit written materials and reports about its operations. The final analysis determined that 22 of the 47 candidates were eligible for further consideration. Table 1.2 lists these 22 candidates (the table also shows the 25 candidates that were considered outside the scope of further interest, and why). From these 22, the study team then selected the final 6, based on the thoroughness of the documentation and accessibility of the site.

Key Lessons. This stage of case study research can assume major proportions within the broader study. In the present illustration, the selection process consumed about 20% of the study's overall resources. Such major

Table 1.2

Organizations Screened by Project Team

Category	Name of Organization Contacted	Location/Belt	Type of Area
I. Within Scope of Further Interest:			
Participation by Local Economic Development Agencies	Chester County Office of Employment and Training*	West Chester, PA/Rustbelt	Rural-Suburban
	City of Grand Rapids Development Office*	Grand Rapids, MI/Rustbelt	Urban-Suburban
	Columbus, Indiana Economic Development Board	Columbus, IN/Rustbelt	Rural
	Corpus Christi Area Economic Development Corporation	Corpus Christi, TX/Sunbelt	Urban
	Department of Community and Senior Citizens Services	Los Angeles, CA/Sunbelt	Suburban
	Department of Economic Development	Tacoma, WA/Mixed	Urban
	Office of Economic and Strategic Development	Merced, CA/Sunbelt	Rural
Participation by Private Industry Councils or JTPA Organizations	Northeast Florida Private Industry Council, Inc.*	Jacksonville, FL/Sunbelt	Rural-Mixed
	Pima County Community Services Department*	Tucson, AZ/Sunbelt	Urban-Rural-Suburban
	Portland Private Industry Council	Portland, OR/Mixed	Urban
	Private Industry Council of Snohomish County	Everett, WA/Mixed	Rural-Suburban
	South Coast Private Industry Council	North Quincy, MA/Snowbelt	Suburban
	Susquehanna Region Private Industry Council, Inc.*	Havre de Grace, MD/Mixed	Rural-Suburban
	Western Missouri Private Industry Council	Sedalia, MO/Mixed	Rural
	Yuma Private Industry Council	Yuma, AZ/Sunbelt	Urban-Towns
Participation by Other Self-Standing Organizations	Cascade Business Center Corporation	Portland, OR/Mixed	Urban
	Daytona Beach Community College	Daytona Beach, FL/Sunbelt	Urban-Rural
	Greater Waterbury Chamber of Commerce	Waterbury, CT/Snowbelt	Towns
	Job Opportunities in Nevada	Reno, NV/Sunbelt	Urban-Rural
	Monadnock Training Council	Milford, NH/Snowbelt	Mixed
	Nevada Business Services	Las Vegas, NV/Sunbelt	Urban
	Seattle-King County Economic Development Council*	Seattle, WA/Mixed	Urban-Suburban

(Continued)

13

Table 1.2
Continued

14

Category	Name of Organization Contacted	Location/Belt	Type of Area
II. Outside Scope of Further Interest:			
Sites With Insufficient	Cambridge Instruments, Inc.	Buffalo, NY/Snowbelt	Urban
Information About	Community College of Rhode island	Lincoln, RI/Snowbelt	Suburban
Economic Development	Frost Incorporated	Grand Rapids, MI/Rustbelt	Urban
Activities	Hawaii Entrepreneurship Training and	Honolulu, HI/Sunbelt	Urban
	Development Institute		
	Indiana Vocational Technical College	Indianapolis, IN/Rustbelt	Mixed
	Metropolitan Re-Employment Project	St. Louis, MO/Rustbelt	Urban
	National Technological University	Ft. Collins, CO/Snowbelt	Mixed
Single Organizations	Coastal Enterprises, Inc.	Wiscasset, ME/Snowbelt	Rural
Operating Both Training	Cooperative Home Care Associates	Bronx, NY/Snowbelt	Urban
and Economic	Esperanza Unida, Inc.	Milwaukee, WI/Snowbelt	Urban
Development Activities	Focus Hope	Detroit, MI/Rustbelt	Urban
	Women's Economic Development Corporation	St. Paul, MN/Snowbelt	Urban-Suburban
Training Institutions	The Business Development and Training Center	Malvern, PA/Rustbelt	Rural
Operating Both Training	at Great Valley		
and Economic	Catonsville Community College	Baltimore, Md./Rustbelt	Urban-Suburban
Development Activities	Highlander Economic Development Center	New Market, TN/Mixed	Rural
	Job Services of Florida	Perry, FL/Sunbelt	Rural
	Luzerne County Community College	Nanticoke, PA/Rustbelt	Urban-Suburban
	Massachusetts Career Development Institute	Springfield, MA/Snowbelt	Suburban
	Niagara County Community College	Sanborn, NY/Snowbelt	Mostly Rural
	Pensacola Junior College	Pensacola, FL/Sunbelt	Metropolitan-Rural
State-Level Operations	Arizona Dept. of Economic Security	Phoenix, AZ/Sunbelt	Mostly Rural
	Bluegrass State Skills Corporation	Frankfort, KY/Mixed	Mixed
	Delaware Development Office	Dover, DE/Rustbelt	Urban-Rural
	State of Iowa Dept. of Economic Development	Des Moines, IA/Snowbelt	Urban-Rural
	North Carolina Department of Community Colleges	Raleigh, NC/Sunbelt	Mixed

* Selected for Case Study

investments are not readily appreciated by funding sponsors. However, if the selection process is not properly conducted, even more trouble will result in the ensuing phases of the research. One option not pursued in this case, but implemented in other studies (e.g., Yin & White, 1986), can make the case selection step even more formal—and produce even more useful information. The option is to define the screening process as a formal survey. Its design would depend on the ability to specify a universe and a sampling plan. However, the survey would provide a broader array of quantitative evidence. The final study would therefore contain limited information on a large number of cases as well as intensive information on a smaller number.

CAUSAL CASE STUDIES I:
FACTOR THEORIES

One of the most common types of causal theories in social science is the *factor* theory (Downs & Mohr, 1976; Mohr, 1978). Whether explaining some economic outcome (marketplace factors), individual behavior (psychological factors), or social phenomenon (social factors), this paradigm assembles some list of independent variables and determines those that are most highly correlated with the dependent variable. Those most highly correlated are then considered causally related to the dependent variable. To conduct the analysis and account for such complexities as the interactions among the independent variables, investigators may use factor analysis, regression analysis, and analysis of variance as illustrative statistical techniques.

The use of factor theories has its counterpart in case study research, although such an application is not desired. However, if factor theories—and not causally linked explanatory theories (see the case after this one)—are the state of the art on a given topic, you may not have the choice of ignoring this application. Many causal case studies have had to be done under these conditions. The following example is therefore included, not only to show how a factor theory could be incorporated into a case study but also to illustrate the limitations of this application.

The Research Issue: How to Attract High-Tech Firms to New Locations. Local economic development theory is a good example of a topic still dominated by factor theories. Firms are said to be influenceable in their decisions to locate or relocate because of the following illustrative types of general factors.

- The availability of venture capital and other forms of start-up financing
- The local tax structure, including costs due to taxes and incentives due to tax breaks
- The physical characteristics of a place (physical capital)
- The labor force characteristics of a place (human capital)
- The governing laws and regulations, covering wages, the formation of unions, depreciation, and numerous other items
- The preferences of key executives and their spouses

Within each general factor can be created long lists of specific factors, and local governments try to use these specific factors as policy tools in attracting firms. The most attractive locale is the one that can maximize as many factors as possible. However, rarely are these factors expressed in some coherent, causal model—which would represent a truly explanatory model of why firms move.

The illustrative study investigated a contemporary offshoot of this traditional situation by focusing on "high-tech" firms (Yin, Sottile, & Bernstein, 1985). The study asked whether high-tech firms respond to the same factors as any industrial firm, or whether some other factors also are important. The study's goal was to identify such distinctive factors, if any, in order to provide advice to local governments desirous of attracting high-tech firms (and not just industrial firms)—a goal glorified by such developmental successes as California's Silicon Valley, North Carolina's Research Triangle, and Boston's Route 128 corridor.

The study could have been designed as a survey or secondary analysis of economic data, which have been common ways of investigating this topic. However, such investigations do not permit in-depth examination of the factors themselves, focusing mainly on the outcome of whether a firm has decided to relocate. In contrast, the illustrative study was intended to examine the factors more closely, thereby requiring data collection from a variety of sources and not just from the firm itself.

Data Collection and Findings From Firms in Nine High-Tech or Industrial Parks. To satisfy this objective, the study team conducted case studies of nine high-tech or industrial parks. The team began with a long list of potential initiatives (or factors) used to attract firms, from the literature. From this long list, the team determined the initiatives (factors) actually used by each park to attract firms, through interviews of the park's developers and local economic development officials as well as through an analysis of documentary evidence. The team then surveyed the firms in each park, to ascertain the firms' rationales for their locational choices and to confirm

Table 1.3

Type of Business Conducted, by Firms in Each Park

Park	Research	Number of Firms, by Type of Business Conducted			
		Light Manufacturing	Heavy Manufacturing and Distribution	Other	Total
A	8	0	0	16	24
B	7	2	0	9	18
C	0	1	8	6	15
D	0	12	6	8	26
E	2	6	3	5	16
F	8	1	0	10	19
G	3	3	3	14	23
H	0	1	2	1	4
I	21	2	0	3	26
Totals	49	28	22	72	171

NOTE: Non-responses = 29
SOURCE: Yin, Sottile, & Bernstein, 1985.

whether these mirrored the parks' initiatives. In all, the team conducted nine case studies and surveyed 200 firms, with responses from 171 of them (86%).

The responses from the firms were initially used to confirm whether the parks were high-tech parks (parks dominated by high-tech firms) or industrial parks (parks dominated by industrial but not high-tech firms). Table 1.3 shows that Parks A, B, F, G, and I had more firms in research businesses than in manufacturing businesses and were therefore considered high-tech parks. Conversely, Parks C, D, E, and H had more firms in manufacturing rather than research businesses and were therefore considered industrial parks.

The case studies were used to determine the initiatives (factors) undertaken by each of the nine parks to attract firms. Overall, certain basic factors (such as location near markets or transportation access) prevailed in all nine parks. However, in comparison to the four industrial parks, the five high-tech parks were found to have undertaken the following additional initiatives:

- Exclusionary zoning or restrictive covenants, to produce a "campuslike" environment
- University initiatives, to create collaborative efforts or personnel exchange between a firm and a local university
- Special utility capabilities, whether related to electrical power or to telephone lines

The identification of these additional initiatives therefore permitted the study team to conclude that high-tech parks had pursued policies distinct from industrial parks. The survey responses from the firms were analyzed to determine whether preference for these same initiatives distinguished high-tech from industrial firms. The results supported, to the acceptable degree of statistical significance, the importance of the university and utility initiatives—but were neutral regarding the importance of a campuslike environment. Despite the neutral confirmation on this last initiative, the study team concluded that jurisdictions wanting to attract high-tech firms should focus on the three initiatives in addition to those used for attracting industrial firms in the first place.

Key Lessons. This example demonstrates the use of a factor theory in a causal case study. The case study was able to identify individual initiatives to attract high-tech firms. Nevertheless, the limitations of this approach also should be evident. Because only a factor theory was available for testing, the following resulted.

• No causal understanding could be developed regarding a firm's actual decision-making process in deciding to relocate.
• The initiatives (or factors) could not be ranked in any order of importance.
• The potential interactions among the factors—and any determination of whether they were part of the same, more general factor—could not be determined.

Possibly the latter two of these shortcomings can be overcome by using some method other than the case study. Factor theories generally thrive when there are sufficient data points to conduct extensive analysis among the factors—thereby favoring survey or secondary analysis rather than case study designs. The ensuing factor analysis or regression analysis could then be directed at determining the relative strength or importance of each factor, as well as at the interactions among the factors. At the same time, even if there are sufficient data points, factor theories are inherently weak in developing an understanding of the underlying causal processes.

CAUSAL CASE STUDIES II:
EXPLANATORY THEORIES

In comparison to factor theories, explanatory theories are more suitable for designing and doing causal case studies. In fact, the more complex and multivariate the explanatory theory, the better. The case study analysis can then take advantage of pattern-matching techniques. Unfortunately, viable explanatory theories do not always exist for the topics covered by case studies, so you cannot always use this approach. However, a study conducted on the topic of research utilization benefited from the prior existence of several complex *and rival* theories—readily translatable into operational terms—and illustrates well the advantages of the approach.

The Research Issue: How and Why Do Research Findings Get Into Practical Use? The illustrative study focused on the key policy objective of making research more useful (Yin & Moore, 1988). Nine case studies were selected in which a funded research project was the unit of analysis. All projects were on a topic of natural hazards research and were known to have been conducted in an exemplary manner—leading to significant scientific publications—but the projects varied in their utilization outcomes. The illustrative study assessed and confirmed these outcomes but then went further to examine the explanations for these outcomes. Such explanations in turn were based on three major rival theories in the literature on research utilization—a knowledge-driven theory, a problem-solving theory, and a social-interaction theory—described next.

The *knowledge-driven theory* stipulates that ideas and discoveries from basic research eventually result in inventions or advances in applied research, often leading to commercial products or services. Utilization is therefore the result of a linear sequence of activities following a "technology-push" process, in which researchers continually produce the new ideas that get put into use.

The *problem-solving theory* also follows a linear sequence. However, the stipulated activities begin with the identification of a problem by some individual or organization—not by a research investigator. Even if the problem has been poorly or incorrectly articulated, it is communicated to a research investigator, whose task is to identify and assess alternative solutions to the problem. The investigator also may redefine the problem. However, utilization is explained by a "demand-pull" process—reflecting the fact that the ultimate user of the research (a) helped to define the initial problem and (b) is therefore waiting for and prepared to implement the solution (assuming a viable one emerges from the research).

The *social-interaction theory* does not stipulate a linear process. Rather, the theory claims that, in high utilization environments, research producers and users belong to overlapping professional networks with ongoing communications. The communications need not focus on any particular research endeavor; rather, the objective of communication is to assure that researchers and users are exposed to each other's worlds and needs—producing a rich "marketplace of ideas" (Yin & Gwaltney, 1981). Such communications can have serendipitous effects. For instance, research investigators may alter the focus of their studies or the early design of their research, based on dialogues with users. Or, as another example, users can project their future needs to reflect a sensitivity to ongoing research developments. In this milieu, utilization ultimately occurs because the continuous flow of communications increasingly leads to good matches between existing needs and emerging new research.

These three theories produced two critical conditions for the illustrative study. First, they led to a predicted and complex course of events when utilization occurs or to the absence of those events when utilization does not occur. The existence of this course of events could then be traced in actual case studies, with a pattern-matching analysis comparing the hypothesized with the actual course (Trochim, 1989; Yin, 1984/1989). The complex nature of the course makes the relevant evidence more discernible. Second, the three theories led to "rival" courses—events that are nearly mutually exclusive. Empirical support for one theory therefore could not be used to argue for support of another theory. In this sense, although the case studies were retrospectively conducted, the data actually permitted the testing of rival theories.

Results. The nine case studies followed a replication design—six cases having strong utilization outcomes although the research covered different academic fields, and three cases having negligible utilization outcomes. The main result was that those cases with the most extensive and diverse array of utilization outcomes were all found to have key ingredients of the social-interaction theory: Existing professional networks created rich, ongoing producer-user dialogue. In some of the cases, professional associations facilitated the exchange of ideas. In other cases, the exchange was simply the result of an active and communicative principal investigator. Overall, communications started earlier than and continued far beyond the ending of a specific research project, in comparison to those projects with minimal utilization outcomes.

Key Lessons. The main lesson from this experience is that the presence of explanatory theories can facilitate theory testing with a rich and extensive data collection effort, including qualitative and quantitative evidence. Each of the nine cases was investigated by reviewing pertinent documents, interviewing a wide array of individuals including actual users of the research, and observing the actual research processes or products. The case study protocol, tightly geared to testing the three theories, assured that the diverse data collection would involve converging lines of inquiry and triangulation of the evidence.

A key aspect of the theories was their complexity. This permitted a pattern-matching of a series or sequence of events as the main analytic tactic in each of the cases. Without the theories or their complexity, data collection might have been undisciplined, and pattern-matching impossible. In this respect, the case study method may rely differently on explanatory theories than do other methods. Whereas other methods may prefer single-variable theories and the incremental development of causal links over a series of studies, the pattern-matching in case study analysis permits case studies to test multiple-variable, complex causal explanations within a single study.

DESCRIPTIVE CASE STUDIES

Rules about the development of descriptive theory have generally been overlooked in favor of rules about explanatory theory (see Box 5). Yet, many investigations have description as their main objective. Such circumstances still call for some theory to determine the priorities for data collection. The typical atheoretic statement "Let's collect information about everything" does not work, and the investigator without a descriptive theory will soon encounter enormous problems in limiting the scope of the study.

Multiple-Case Design. An illustrative use of descriptive theory was a study on "special education"—education for students with disabilities—in four states (Massachusetts, South Dakota, North Dakota, and New Jersey; Pyecha et al., 1988). The case study analysis followed a pattern-matching procedure: Data about each state's activities were compared to two rival, idealized, and theoretic patterns. The prediction was that two of the states (Massachusetts and South Dakota) would follow one pattern but not the other, whereas the other two states (North Dakota and New Jersey) would have the reverse result.

Thus the case study design, even for a descriptive study, followed a replication logic. Without sufficiently strong theory, the differences or similarities among the states would be difficult to interpret. In other words, the role of theory was to specify the differences between the two types of states that would be considered substantively critical. The key to the study

---

BOX 5
"Theories" for Descriptive Case Studies

References to the use of "theory" usually involve the formation of hypotheses of cause-effect relationships. These theories would therefore be considered relevant to explanatory case studies.

"Theories," however, also can be important for descriptive case studies. A descriptive theory is not an expression of a cause-effect relationship. Rather, a descriptive theory covers the scope and depth of the object (case) being described. If you were to describe an individual, an organization, or some other possible subject of a case study, where should your description start, and where should it end? What should your description include, and what might be excluded? The criteria used to answer these questions would represent your "theory" of what needs to be described. This theory should be openly stated ahead of time, should be subject to review and debate, and will later serve as the "design" for a descriptive case study. The more thoughtful the theory, the better the descriptive case study will be.

---

design was the detailed development of the rival theoretic patterns, portrayed as alternative "scenarios." Experts helped to develop and review these scenarios—or descriptive theories—against which the actual data were compared.

The Research Issue: Categorical Versus Noncategorical Education. Elementary and secondary schooling for students with disabilities commonly occurs in *categorical,* self-contained classes. In this arrangement, students are first categorized according to their disability, and those with similar disabilities are grouped and taught together for some if not all of their classes. This philosophy of education argues that (a) different disabilities arise from different etiologies; (b) students with different disabilities have different learning needs; and therefore (c) different instructional methods must be developed and tailored to each type of disability. Further, grouping the students according to their disabilities leads to more homogeneous classrooms, making teaching easier.

As logical as the argument appears, an alternative educational philosophy is that the educational needs and learning processes of disabled students are basically no different from each other or from those without disabilities. Differences may arise in the level of a student's achievement, but separate instructional methods are not relevant. Thus except for limited supplemental situations, students with and without disabilities should share the same classrooms and curriculum.

This alternative philosophy is known as *noncategorical* education, whose implementation brings different features in comparison to categorical systems. First and foremost, a noncategorical system permits the disabled student to remain in his or her neighborhood school, whereas categorical systems can lead to special classes (indeed, special schools) in remote locations. Second, a noncategorical system is fully integrated with the regular education system, whereas a categorical system produces a dual system (one for regular students and the other for handicapped students). Third, a noncategorical system avoids the potential negative consequences of "labeling" a student with a disability.

Debate over these contrasting philosophies has been strong. Current federal policy tends to favor the development of categorical systems, but states are the ones charged with delivering public education services and must therefore design their own policies. During the past decade, only two states have chosen to implement noncategorical systems—Massachusetts and South Dakota. A study of how such systems differ, in practice, from categorical systems had to be conceived as a case study.

The purpose of the study was not to determine which system was better. Instead, the purpose was descriptive—to define current practices in using noncategorical systems, determining whether such practices are indeed different from those in categorical systems.

Units of Analysis and Selection of Cases. Because state policy is the organizing force for all local public education, the state was the main unit of analysis. The study had to include Massachusetts and South Dakota automatically, because they were the only states with noncategorical systems. For comparison purposes, the study team selected two geographically similar states to be paired with these first two states—New Jersey for Massachusetts, and North Dakota for South Dakota.

Within each state, educational services are delivered by local systems. Among the four states, 28 such local systems were therefore also selected for study, representing an embedded unit of analysis. The data from the local systems were needed to assure that differences in state policies actually resulted in different practices at the local level. For this reason, the selection of these 28 local systems was based on a state official's informed judgment that a district was implementing the state's policies with fidelity. The selection of local systems therefore again reflected a replication logic.

Development of Descriptive Scenarios. The design of the study required the careful development of idealized scenarios of the two types of systems.

Draft scenarios were initially based on the research literature and consultation with experts. An expert advisory panel then reviewed the drafts, making important comments and modifications. The completed scenarios became the basis for developing data collection protocols.

The importance of these scenarios within the study design cannot be underestimated. Descriptive studies typically fail to specify a priori the critical ingredients of the phenomenon to be described. Data collection then rambles as a result, and the ensuing case study may even contain undesirable, circular reasoning—the final description constituting a contaminated combination of what might have been expected and what was found. In contrast, the scenarios were intended to recapture the essence of what constituted categorical or noncategorical systems. The driving question underlying the development of the scenarios was, "What features must a school system have in order for it to be considered an example of categorical (or noncategorical) education?" Only after these scenarios were completed could data collection begin. Confirming or disconfirming evidence on both scenarios was sought in all four states.

You should note that, under this scheme, unanticipated findings are still not precluded. Revelatory or important information found outside of the original scenario can still be collected and analyzed later. However, the initial scenarios provide major support in structuring the data collection in the first place and avoiding an unending collection process.

Illustrative Results. The study team collected data from four states and 28 local systems. Tables 1.4 and 1.5 show a portion of the results, focusing on propositions about categorical and noncategorical systems, respectively. The numbers reflect the number of local systems in each state in which the proposition was supported, refuted, or neither support nor refuted (S-R-N). The two tables show that for many propositions the school systems in the four states followed the predicted patterns. The exceptions were mainly among the items related to teaching and administration, due to the fact that all school systems must attempt to implement certain uniform policies. Because of the strong contrasts among the items for student assessment and placement, however, the overall results were considered as following the predicted pattern. Further, the two states with categorical policies were generally more like each other than like the two states with noncategorical policies. The overall pattern of results was then used to describe how noncategorical systems differ from categorical systems.

Key Lessons. One lesson was that the scenarios could not have been developed had there not been a rich literature and policy debate on

Table 1.4

Propositions About Categorical Systems

	Proposition Number	Local District Patterns				
		Categorical States		Noncategorical States		
Proposition		New Jersey	North Dakota	Massachusetts	South Dakota
		S-R-N[a]	S-R-N[a]	S-R-N[a]	S-R-N[a]
Student Assessment and Placement:					
Eligibility is based on identification of handicapping condition	C5	8-0-0	6-0-0	1-7-0	1-5-0
Students are placed in categorical classes	C9	1-5-2	3-0-3	0-6-2	0-4-2
Assessment focuses on handicapping condition	C4	8-0-0	6-0-0	1-6-1	3-3-0
IEPs differ along categorical lines	C7	5-2-1	6-0-0	0-8-0	2-4-0
For cross-categorical classes, groupings are categorical	C12	0-8-0	0-6-0	0-8-0	0-6-0
Teaching and Administration:					
Teaching methods suit handicapping condition	C13	2-5-1	6-0-0	0-8-0	1-4-1
Each handicapping condition has its own curriculum	C15	3-5-0	0-1-5	0-8-0	0-6-0
LEA staffs are organized categorically	C22	0-8-0	3-0-3	1-6-1	1-4-1
Vertical communications are categorical	C23	0-6-2	3-3-0	0-7-1	1-4-1
Special education is located in special facilities	C24	1-4-3	0-6-0	0-4-4	0-5-1

NOTE: a. The three numbers indicate the number of districts for which the proposition or assumption was supported, refuted, or neither supported nor refuted. Example: "4-3-1" means that the proposition was supported in four districts, refuted in three, and mixed (neither supported nor refuted) in one. IEP: Individualized Education Program. LEA: Local Education Agency.

Table 1.5
Propositions About Noncategorical Systems

		Local District Patterns			
		Categorical States		Noncategorical States	
Proposition	Proposition Number	New Jersey	North Dakota	Massachusetts	South Dakota
		S-R-N[a]	S-R-N[a]	S-R-N[a]	S-R-N[a]
Student Assessment and Placement:					
Every school has noncategorical resource room	N9	0-8-0	0-6-0	8-0-0	4-2-0
Placement is to home/neighborhood school	N10	0-8-0	0-6-0	6-1-1	3-3-0
Eligibility is based on progress in regular curriculum	N5	0-8-0	0-6-0	7-1-0	5-1-0
Identification of handicapping condition is not needed	N6	0-8-0	0-6-0	7-1-0	5-1-0
Academic tests prevail over all other types of tests	N4	0-8-0	1-5-0	5-0-3	4-2-0
IEPs contain academic benchmarks	N7	0-6-2	0-4-2	5-2-1	2-2-2
Placement decisions are based on regular curriculum	N11	0-8-0	0-6-0	8-0-0	4-1-1
Exit criteria are based on regular curriculum	N20	8-0-0	6-0-0	8-0-0	4-1-1
Groupings are like those of regular education	N14	7-0-1	6-0-0	8-0-0	5-1-0
Teaching and Administration:					
Teaching techniques are like regular education	N16	8-0-0	6-0-0	8-0-0	6-0-0
Neighborhood school staff can do needed academic testing	N3	4-4-0	6-0-0	8-0-0	6-0-0
Regular curriculum is used in special education classes	N18	2-0-6	1-1-4	2-1-5	2-1-3
Special and regular education undertake joint activities	N22	3-3-2	5-1-0	3-3-2	4-2-0
LEA and SEA special education staffs are organized by function	N23	8-0-0	0-3-3	6-1-1	4-1-1
Flexibility is allowed in teacher assignments	N24	7-1-0	1-5-0	7-0-1	4-0-2
Principals control special education in schools	N26	1-7-1	2-3-1	0-8-0	1-5-0
Special and regular education staffs work cooperatively	N28	2-3-3	4-1-1	4-1-3	4-1-1

NOTE: a. The three numbers indicate the number of districts for which the proposition or assumption was supported, refuted, or neither supported nor refuted. Example: "4-3-1" means that the proposition was supported in four districts, refuted in three, and mixed (neither supported nor refuted) in one. IEP: Individualized Education Program. LEA: Local Education Agency. SEA = State Education Agency.

categorical versus noncategorical systems. The literature and debate provided an array of contrasts, in highly operational terms, to be tested in the field. Many other topics of interest to researchers may not have such rich sources, and the descriptive theory cannot be developed as easily before a case study is to be done. Under such circumstances, the final result may border on an exploratory rather than descriptive case study. A second lesson concerned the benefit from having rival theories. Without the categorical system as a contrast, any description of the noncategorical system could have become undisciplined and spilled over to other aspects of school system operations not critical to their noncategorical nature. The availability of a rival theory helped to avoid such an expansive tendency and instead focused data collection on the features important to noncategorical systems.

CONCLUSIONS

These five illustrations show the multiple applications of theory to case study research and evaluations. Critical to all the illustrations was the development of such theory prior to the conduct of the study. Further, such development frequently required substantial time, resources, and substantive expertise.

This approach to case studies mimics that used in most experimental science, where expert knowledge of prior research and careful hypothesis development precede actual experimentation. The approach therefore requires you to be well informed about the topics of inquiry and not simply to have a methodological tool kit. Moreover, the approach gives you an opportunity to reveal (and minimize) substantive biases that may affect the design and conduct of your case study. Finally, the approach produces case studies that can be part of a cumulative body of knowledge rather than just isolated empirical inquiries.

EXERCISES

1. *Three kinds of theories.* Describe the differences among three types of theories: exploratory theories, descriptive theories, and explanatory theories. Can you give examples of each, where the subject of study might be the same?

2. *Studying routinization.* Name other situations in which the issue of routinization is relevant. Are they all situations in which the case study method would be the method of choice for conducting a study?

3. *Screening potential cases.* Name a topic of study of interest to you, in which the case study method was the likely method of choice. What candidate sites or examples would you consider as possible cases? How would you screen these sites or examples?

4. *Studying how research findings get into practical use.* Name some examples where research has (eventually) led to practical results. Could you use the case study method to investigate these examples? How would you define the case, and what would be your study questions?

5. *Case studies in special education.* Name different topics in special education that might lead to case study investigations. Are these topics about individual students? About classroom activities or instruction? About special education programs?

PART II

Design and Analysis

2

Case Study Design in Educational Research

DEFINITION OF THE CASE STUDY METHOD AND IMPORTANCE OF CASE STUDY DESIGNS

Case studies are an appropriate research method when you are trying to attribute causal relationships—and not just wanting to explore or describe a situation. As pointed out in Chapter 1, the major rationale for using this method is when your investigation must cover both a particular *phenomenon* and the *context* within which the phenomenon is occurring, either because (a) the context is hypothesized to contain important explanatory variables about the phenomenon or (b) the boundaries between phenomenon and context are not clearly evident.

Chapter 1 presented a major application of case studies in education, covering a topic on state education systems. Other examples in education include a curriculum practice (phenomenon) as part of the larger curriculum—formal and informal (context); student-teacher interactions in a classroom (phenomenon) as part of a school's tradition, neighborhood setting, and district policies (context); and student performance (phenomenon) as part of the student's peer environment, family interactions, and prior experience with schooling (context). To take a more dramatic example, the massive decentralization of Chicago's schools (phenomenon)—initiated in 1988—can only be appreciated in the context of the Chicago system's history of poor performance and nonresponsive policies (context).

Put simply, the context is extremely relevant in many educational situations. However, as soon as this is acknowledged, a major problem arises: The contextual variables are so numerous and rich that no experimental design can be applied. (In fact, experimental designs typically "control out" context and focus only on phenomenon; experiments therefore work best

AUTHOR'S NOTE: This is an expanded and adapted version of "Case Study Design" by Marvin C. Alkin in *Encyclopedia of Educational Research* (6th ed., pp. 134-137). Copyright © 1992 by American Educational Research Association. Used by permission of Macmillan Publishing Company.

when you are focusing only on a specific variable or two, in isolation from the broader environment or context.) Further, the contextual variables may be so qualitatively different that no single survey or data collection approach can be used to collect the information about these variables. The analytic result of being concerned with context is to introduce a large number of variables into a study, with this number likely to exceed by far the number of data points available. The case study may therefore be technically defined as:

> An empirical inquiry in which the number of variables exceeds the number of data points.

Moreover, this definition pertains regardless of the data collection methods being used.

In fact, a point of confusion in the past has been the unfortunate linking between the case study method and certain types of data collection—for example, those focusing on qualitative methods, ethnography, or participant-observation (see Chapter 4). People have thought that the case study method required them to embrace these data collection methods if they were to do case studies at all. On the contrary, the method does not imply any particular form of data collection—which can be qualitative or quantitative (Yin, 1984/1989, pp. 24-25). The important aspect of case study data collection is the use of multiple sources of evidence—converging on the same set of issues. As for designs, the case study is a method with its own designs and analytic routines, differentiating it from other methods. The most compelling designs are those attempting to test rival educational theories—using single or multiple cases. The complete design also will specify the case selection criteria (see the illustrative application in Chapter 1) and the logic for the basic data collection strategies.

DESIGN ISSUES FOR CASE STUDIES IN EDUCATION

Many investigators believe that once the case study has been selected as the method to be used, the investigator's major remaining responsibility is to "enter the field" and to start collecting data. In fact, much work needs to be done before data collection begins. Four design issues are especially important (see Box 6 for more on "method" versus "design").

First, you must try to identify the major unit of analysis for the case study. As noted in Chapter 1, the question here is, "What is the 'case'?" Educational research offers many possibilities, of which those listed here

---

BOX 6

The Case Study as a Method Versus Case Study Designs

For doing empirical research, a complete method should specify the conditions for (a) designing an investigation, (b) collecting the pertinent data, (c) analyzing the data, and (d) reporting the findings. A prior textbook (Yin, 1984/1989) has presented the case study as a "method," by covering all of these topics.

Within the case study method, you must therefore attend to these four components. The present book (as well as the prior textbook) gives more advice on the design component than any of the others, following the belief that previous texts have overemphasized data collection procedures and underemphasized design.

When you focus on case study "designs," you are mainly dealing with the logic whereby initial hypotheses or research questions can be subjected to empirical testing. Deciding between single- or multiple-case studies, selecting the specific cases to be studied, developing a case study protocol, and defining the relevant data collection strategies—for example, the relevant time period to be covered by the data collection—are all part of a case study design. However, how the data are actually collected will be part of the data collection component, not the design.

In this manner, the case study method is presented as a full-fledged method for conducting research. Case study designs are considered one component of this method.

---

are but a few: (a) a student or a teacher, (b) a classroom or class, (c) a school, (d) a curriculum, (e) a teaching practice, or (f) a decision about a school policy. Once defined, the unit of analysis (or "case") provides stability to a case study design. Simple designs can have single units of analysis; more complicated designs can have multiple units, embedded within each other (e.g., a school might be the main single case, but an embedded unit of analysis might be the students in the school). When an embedded design is used, different research questions and instruments are needed for each unit of analysis.

Second, you should decide whether a single case or multiple cases are to be the subject of study. Case study research can rightfully cover both situations. If a single case, the case can serve exploratory, descriptive, or even causal purposes—the last being possible if the case is a "critical" case, in which the empirical data are used to test an important theory. If multiple cases, the logic bringing the cases together should be considered a *replication* logic rather than any *sampling* logic—see Box 7 (Yin, 1984/ 1989, pp. 53-58). Thus two or three cases might be chosen in the hopes

---

BOX 7
Replication, Not Sampling Logic, for Multiple-Case Studies

Multiple-case studies should follow a replication, not sampling logic. This means that two or more cases should be included within the same study precisely because the investigator predicts that similar results (replications) will be found. If such replications are indeed found for several cases, you can have more confidence in the overall results. The development of consistent findings, over multiple cases and even multiple studies, can then be considered a very robust finding.

Sampling logics are entirely different. They assume that an investigation is mainly interested in "representing" a larger universe. The cases selected are therefore chosen according to pre-identified representation criteria. These logics do not work well with multiple-case studies and in fact distort the benefits of using the case study method in the first place. In fact, if the sampling logic is important to an inquiry, the survey or experimental methods are more likely to satisfy an investigation's needs than is the case study method.

---

of replicating a certain finding. The more replications, the more robust your findings will be. (A sampling logic would be a situation in which the cases were considered data points from some larger universe. However, this would be an inappropriate rationale, because the case study results are not to be generalized to a population but rather to some theory.)

Third, you must specify how the single or multiple cases are to be selected. Your selection criteria may include the following.

- Criticality for the theory being tested—for example, some case is a "critical" case
- Topical relevance—for example, some case is best for the phenomenon being studied
- Feasibility and access—for example, some person or group is willing to be the subject of a case study

Whatever the criteria, the case selection process can itself be lengthy and involved. You may have to collect preliminary information from a large number of preliminary candidates, and then perform a screening analysis, to determine the final candidates (also see Chapter 1 for an extended application). Under these circumstances, you must avoid allowing the screening process to become so extensive that it effectively becomes a study in itself.

Fourth, you may choose between at least two different data collection strategies, or you deliberately may choose to use both: a one-time data collection effort (typically, a small number of days for every case to be studied), in which only post-hoc longitudinal data can be collected; or a more extended data collection period (typically, a year or more for each case), in which true longitudinal data can be collected (see Chapter 3). The first mode is not likely to permit direct, on-site observations of key events; much of the critical information must be collected through interviews and documents. The second mode is more costly and requires special access to educational facilities; however, this mode does permit direct observations—but you are not likely to have any control over whether the relevant events will reliably occur or not, and if they do, whether you will happen to be at the right place at the right time to observe them.

AN EXAMPLE: EDUCATIONAL PARTNERSHIPS

Partnerships between schools and other organizations—that is, other public agencies and private businesses—have become one strategic policy approach for improving educational outcomes. These partnerships are reflected in school-business consortia, "adopt-a-school" programs, and more complicated community efforts. If you are doing case studies of these partnerships, you would have to confront the preceding four design issues. Therefore, the partnership case studies provide an illustrative example of these four issues. (For a related application, also see the application covering interorganizational partnerships in Chapter 1.)

First, Figure 2.1 suggests that the unit of analysis for studying the partnership is indeed the partnership itself—which is far different from defining the unit of analysis as one of the collaborating organizations. However, as the unit of analysis, a "partnership" is an abstract concept and therefore can be difficult to study. For instance, every partnership can be seen as having its own activities and outcomes, and these should represent a collectivity greater than the sum of the activities and outcomes carried out singly by the participating organizations.

Figure 2.1 further suggests that the partnership activities themselves might be considered as having "partnership" outcomes and the education activities also would be considered as having education outcomes. However, an oversight in the past has been the attempt to oversimplify these combinations and to assume that the partnership activities produce educational outcomes directly (see "Process-Outcome" Framework in Figure 2.1).

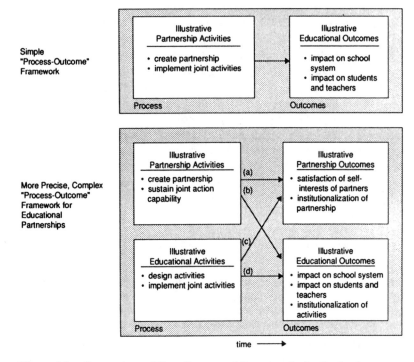

Figure 2.1. Comparison of Two Conceptual Frameworks for Evaluating Educational Partnerships

Second, Figure 2.2 shows how you might incorporate multiple- and not just single-case studies as part of your study. The figure points to the possibility of multiple partnerships, at different points of maturation. All of these partnerships could be made part of the same study.

Third, Figure 2.2 provides a clue regarding the criteria for selecting the multiple cases. A screening process would be needed to identify different partnerships at different points of maturation, but such a process would not be a difficult undertaking.

Fourth, you would still need to decide between a one-time data collection effort and a more extended period in which true longitudinal data would be collected. Your decision between these two modes of data collection would depend on the specific partnership questions being studied and the opportunities and access provided in the field. However, in summary, the study of educational partnerships provides a good example of how

Complex
Process-Outcome
Framework

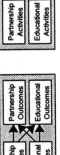
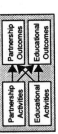
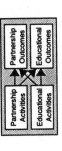
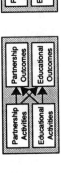

| Partnership Activities | Partnership Outcomes |
| Educational Activities | Educational Outcomes |

Startup Stage
of Partnership

Growth Stage
of Partnership

Mature Stage
of Partnership

Institutionalized Stage
of Partnership

Illustrative
Evaluation
Questions

Startup Stage of Partnership
- Was the partnership started from internal or external forces?
- Did the partnership use a strategic planning process to set partnership and educational goals?
- How were the initial educational activities identified?

Growth Stage of Partnership
- Did the partnership identify resources for growth?
- Were partnership agreements formalized and staff resources settled?
- Were there initial, incremental successes?
- Did the educational activities broaden the partnership's constituency?

Mature Stage of Partnership
- Did the partnership serve the self-interests of the partners?
- Did the partnership survive initial staff and resource turnover?
- Did the partnership produce visible educational results?
- Did the partnership attain broad community support?

Institutionalized Stage of Partnership
- Has the partnership survived turnover of key partner representatives?
- Is partnership empowerment occurring?
- Does resource infusion come from an institutionalized source?
- Have educational activities been successfully repeated?
- Have key educational outcomes been repeated?

Figure 2.2. Life Cycle Framework for Evaluating Educational Partnerships

37

choices in case study design must reflect the substantive objectives of a study as well as the characteristics of the topic being studied.

THE ROLE OF THEORY AND HYPOTHESIS-TESTING

As seen in Chapter 1, among the most important additional aspects of design is the role of theory and hypothesis-testing—even if a case study is to be exploratory or descriptive, but certainly if it is to be an investigation of causal relationships.

A theory is simply an a priori explanation of why some educational phenomenon might have occurred the way it did. The explanation is causal in the sense that it identifies cause-and-effect relationships among a series of events, with each relationship being expressed as a hypothesis. The causal chain also must conclude with some measurable outcome. For example, a common theory about learning in the classroom is that the critical ingredient is "time on task" or "academic learning time." Moreover, this ingredient was overlooked in earlier studies, which focused only on the substantive aspects of a curriculum and not necessarily on the time spent on educational tasks. Assessing "time on task" is therefore claimed to explain the outcomes of many educational initiatives. Similarly, a common theory about implementing educational change is that "mutual adaptation" occurs, in which the innovative idea and the school setting both undergo change during implementation, the final outcome being a distinctive combination of practices (Berman & McLaughlin, 1976; McLaughlin, 1976).

Case studies designed to examine these theories would specify the operational chain of events leading to the relevant outcomes. The important steps in the design process would be to (a) specify the outcomes of concern; (b) reference existing causal theories—or develop a new one—in enumerating "how" and "why" questions to explain the outcomes; (c) decompose these questions into a series of causally linked hypotheses; and (d) develop operational definitions of the outcomes and the hypotheses.

In contrast, a poorly specified theory—in terms of cause-and-effect relationships—would be a *factor* theory (also see Chapter 1 for an extended application). School effectiveness theory (e.g., Brookover, 1981; Cohen, 1982) is a factor theory. The theory specifies the correlates of school effectiveness but does not explain how to attain the outcomes of interest. This type of theory would therefore not provide a solid foundation for case study research, because you would not know the sequence of events being tested. Enumerating the frequency with which the key factors were encountered would likely favor some other methodology, such as a regression analysis.

In other words, the correct specification of a theory will provide you with a predicted pattern of events. This pattern then becomes a series of benchmarks against which actual data can be compared. In this way, you can test a theory even with empirical evidence collected from a single case study—the analytic process being a "pattern-matching" process (Yin, 1984/1989, pp. 109-113).

An even stronger design would specify two or more rival theories, leading to mutually exclusive patterns. The data collection from a single case could then be examined to determine which pattern was more valid. In a well-known education case study of this sort, Gross et al. (1971) showed that a *barrier* theory of innovation did not explain the innovative outcome at a single elementary school, but that an *implementation* theory did. In other words, a single case study was the basis for testing rival theories. (At the individual student level, any number of studies in which behavioral and Piagetian theories of learning were put forth as rivals could be designed.)

The specification of a theory serves yet another important purpose in doing case study research. The theory becomes the vehicle for generalizing the results of the case study. In other words, rather than generalizing to a universe or population, case study research should be used to expand our understanding of theoretical propositions and hypotheses in those situations where (a) the context is important and (b) events cannot be manipulated (as in an experiment). These are common situations in educational research, and therefore the case study method is widely applicable to such research.

TESTS OF VALIDITY AND RELIABILITY

A final consideration in case study designs is to create designs with construct validity, internal validity, external validity, and reliability (Yin, 1984/1989, pp. 40-45).

Construct validity deals with the use of instruments and measures that accurately operationalize the constructs of interest in a study. Because most instruments and measures are not necessarily as accurate as desired, a common strategy is to use multiple measures of the same construct as part of the same study. This same strategy works well in designing case

studies and has been defined as the use of multiple sources of evidence (Yin, 1984/1989, p. 23).

Both *internal validity* and *external validity* were touched on in the discussion on the role of theory. You can achieve internal validity through the specification of the units of analysis, the development of a priori rival theories, and the collection and analysis of data to test these rivals. Similarly, you can achieve external validity through the specification of theoretical relationships, from which generalizations can then be made.

Finally, you can achieve *reliability* through the use of formal case study protocols and the development of a case study database. The protocols especially help to ensure that the same procedures are followed in multiple cases or in a study conducted by multiple investigators. The case study database is a way of differentiating the evidence from the case study manuscript. These two components are readily differentiated in other methods —for example, a survey database as distinct from the survey report—but are often confused in traditional uses of the case study.

CONCLUSIONS: CASE STUDIES IN EDUCATION

Among educators, the case study remains an unappreciated and under-utilized research tool. Most people use it as a method of last resort, and even then they use it with uneasiness and uncertainty. Despite the availability of key works on how to do case study research (e.g., U.S. General Accounting Office, 1987; Yin, 1984/1989), this practice has been reinforced by the lack of attention to the method in many textbooks. For instance, in the 5th edition of their widely used textbook on evaluation research, Rossi and Freeman (1993) still do not mention case studies as a form of inquiry of any sort. Similarly, the 5th edition of the well-known *Research Methods in Social Relations* (Kidder et al., 1986) contains only a single reference to case studies—covering the outdated and limited role of the "one-shot" case study as a "pre-experimental" design.

Yet, case studies have frequently been the method of choice among experienced investigators in education for analyzing (a) educational innovations (Gross et al., 1971), (b) implementation of federal aid-to-education policy (McLaughlin, 1975), (c) excellence in high schools (Lightfoot, 1983; Yin & White, 1986), and (d) the uses of evaluation findings in education (Alkin et al., 1979). These and other examples of the use of case studies have produced important data and ideas and have helped to advance educational research.

Case studies also form a database for further refining both methodological and substantive issues. Therefore, new investigators may want to develop a better understanding of when and how to use the case study method. The purpose of this chapter has been to provide such an understanding. The chapter has emphasized the design phase in doing case studies. Guidance on data collection, data analysis, and reporting methods can be found in other sources (e.g., Merriam, 1988), as case studies share many of these techniques with other methods. However, case study design is distinctive to the case study method—serving as the most challenging and unique aspect of doing case studies. Consequently, you should spend considerable time and resources on the design phase and especially should not rush into data collection.

A final note is that case study designs also are dynamic, in that the original design may have to undergo any number of "redesigns." You may even have to change designs after data collection has started. For instance, during data collection, you may realize that the original definitions and objectives are not as relevant as newly discovered items. In such situations, redesign should be seriously considered. However, redesign means scrapping the original design and specifying a new one; redesign does not mean that you can incrementally alter a case study inquiry as data are being collected—a practice that has led to a major criticism of case study research (Yin, Bateman, & Moore, 1985).

If the preceding suggestions for case study designs are followed, you are more likely to use the case study method successfully, and educational research will advance in significant and perhaps unanticipated ways.

EXERCISES

1. *Using case studies in educational research.* Identify one or more case studies in educational research. Classify the study(ies) according to: (a) the unit of analysis (student, classroom, school, etc.); (b) the topic of educational theory (classroom management, educational technology, school effectiveness or excellence, etc.); and (c) whether single- or multiple-case studies were part of the inquiry.

2. *Including phenomenon and context in an educational study.* Think about designing a case study of an educational phenomenon. What is the phenomenon to be studied? What is the context within which the phenomenon occurs? Within your hypothetical study, name some subtopics where the boundary between

phenomenon and context are blurred, in contrast to some in which the boundary is sharp.

3. *Selecting the individual cases to be studied.* In your hypothetical study in Question 2 above, name several actual, concrete examples of the cases you would include in the study. By what criteria did you select these cases? Are the criteria related to the hypotheses of study, to opportunistic conditions, or to some other consideration?

4. *Redesigning an educational case study.* Assume you started a real case study of some educational phenomenon. Name some conditions that you might have encountered—that would lead to your redesigning your entire case study.

3

Research Design Issues in Using the Case Study Method to Study Management Information Systems

THE GENERAL ROLE OF RESEARCH DESIGNS

The study of management information systems presents another application for using the case study method. As in doing educational research, you may think that selecting the case study method has resolved a major problem. You may think that you can proceed directly into the "field," where you can start collecting real-life data, and that all you need to do is to identify a "willing site"—that is, one in which you can conduct interviews, make observations, and generally hang around. If the site is a neighborhood or public place, work can start almost immediately. If the site is an organization—which is more likely to be the case in the study of management information systems (MIS)—you may face a major hurdle in gaining permission (Hedrick, Bickman, & Rog, 1993), but this is frequently perceived as the only hurdle to be surmounted before commencing the case study (see Box 8). (For business organizations especially, the problem of gaining access can be a serious problem—and naturally draws considerable attention in preparing to do a study; see also Maruyama & Deno, 1992.)

Nothing could be more misleading than the preceding scenario. In fact, most types of case studies require an extensive degree of preparation and homework, involving attempts to answer such questions as these:

- How are you going to define your case?
- Are you doing a single- or multiple-case study? If multiple, should they be done sequentially or in parallel; and if sequentially, in what order?

AUTHOR'S NOTE: This chapter is an expanded and adapted version of an article of the same name appearing in James I. Cash and Paul R. Lawrence (Eds.), *The Information Systems Research Challenge: Qualitative Research Methods* (pp. 1-6). Boston: Harvard Business School, 1989. Used by permission of the publisher.

BOX 8
A Growing Interest in Case Study Research on the Part of
Business Schools

Business schools have been the bastion of the case study as a *teaching* tool. The Harvard "case method" has long been famous for its benefits in exposing students to hypothetical, real-life situations for teaching purposes. Other business schools and departments in other disciplines have similarly used the case study teaching method to good advantage.

Recently, business schools have witnessed a resurgence of interest in the case study, but as a *research* strategy. Although business faculty and students have always conducted empirical research projects, such projects are becoming increasingly common, and the case study has become valued as one of the possible research strategies. The Harvard Business School has been active in this area, as reflected by the present chapter. The self-acclaimed "Harvard" of Canada—the University of Western Ontario Business School —also has seen case study research proliferate. Finally, even students in Europe—such as those matriculating at Denmark's Aarhus School of Business—also have participated in this resurgence.

Asked to give one reason to account for the popularity of the method, one Harvard professor discussed current research on management information systems (MISs). He noted that, whereas traditional MIS systems were simply a subfunction of an organization, the newer MISs could potentially lead to the restructuring of the entire organization, with the firm in its entirety becoming an MIS. He went on to observe that only the case study method could capture such dynamic, changing conditions.

- How should the case be bounded with regard to time, participants, and relevant evidence? If, for instance, you are studying an organization, should you try to interview key officials who might have left the organization several years ago?
- What are you seeking to prove, conclude, or observe?
- How should you decide whom to interview and how long the interviews should be? What type of interview instrument, if any, should you use?
- How should you deal with other sources of evidence, and what happens if events change drastically during the case? Do you need to start over again?
- Finally, what should you do with your notes and other materials when you are ready to "write up" the case?

A case study should not begin until these questions have been addressed. Furthermore, you should not be surprised to find that many organizations have become accustomed to being the subjects of management and organizational studies—and themselves will want to know the answers to most of these questions before granting you access to their staff and facilities. Finally, few research sponsors are willing to make awards without answers to these kinds of questions.

Case studies of MISs, therefore, provide yet another example of the importance of case study designs. Remember that a good research design should deal specifically with the preceding questions. The research design is a technical plan (as distinguished from a management plan, which deals with the resources, logistics, scheduling and assignment of personnel, and other tasks involved in administering a research project) that attempts to link the beginning and ending of a study, helping the investigator get "from here (the beginning) to there (the ending)." Technically, the role of a research design is to assure that the evidence to be collected is pertinent to the questions of study and that the analytic strategies cover the critical rival hypotheses or competing concerns of a case study. Note that the design is a logic plan, connecting the study questions with data collection and interpretation and conclusions—not just a logistics plan (which also may be needed).

Although its role has usually been underestimated, a well-articulated research design may be one of the most important ingredients in doing a good case study. Although a case study—unlike other types of empirical inquiries—may not boast a fully articulated design at its outset because the design may be subject to modification as the study progresses, you are nevertheless well advised to have as thorough a research design as possible, as early as possible.

A good research design should force you to do the following:

- Articulate the objectives and questions of study, and show how the method to be used bears on these objectives or questions (e.g., the case study method is not appropriate for all objectives or questions).
- Link the objectives and questions to the basic unit of study (e.g., a single case or multiple cases).
- Identify the critical evidence—interviews, documentation, and observations—that will support the major hypotheses of study, including the potentially contrary evidence that would support rival hypotheses.
- Stipulate the relevant techniques for analyzing the evidence, so that the questions of initial interest are addressed in a critical manner.
- Provide clear direction for one of the most vexing problems of case studies —generalizing from the results to other cases (Yin, Bateman, & Moore, 1985).

How to create good research designs remains an "art" that most investigators improve on throughout their entire careers. At the present time, there exists no specific training, manual, or "cookbook" from which this art might be effectively derived, though some guidelines have been identified (Yin, 1984/1989). The purpose here is to consider only a few of the more common design choices that you will face—especially in doing research on MISs.

CASE STUDY RESEARCH VERSUS ETHNOGRAPHIC RESEARCH

The first choice that needs to be made is between two rather different approaches to the study of MISs in organizations. Although both involve fieldwork and seemingly similar activities, they are based on drastically different premises. A more extensive discussion is also presented in Chapter 4. For MIS research, the key issues are as follows.

The case study approach may be characterized as seeking (a) to define specific questions of study ahead of time, (b) to emulate logical positivism (see Box 9) in developing rival hypotheses and collecting external evidence bearing on these questions, and (c) to carry out fieldwork in a targeted fashion—that is, focusing on the evidence deemed relevant and doing the fieldwork in a time-limited fashion. The present chapter is based on this approach, which has been practiced frequently in MIS research (e.g., Benbasat, Goldstein, & Mead, 1987; George & McKeown, 1985; Kling & Iacono, 1984; Lee, 1988; Leonard-Barton, 1987; Markus, 1983).

In contrast, an ethnographic approach may be characterized as one in which the investigation seeks to (Fetterman, 1989) (a) gain a close-up, detailed rendition ("thick description") of the real world; (b) challenge the logical positivist position by claiming that all evidence is relative and therefore cannot be independent of the investigator—thereby favoring participant-observation (Jorgensen, 1989) as the dominant mode of data collection; and (c) permit and even encourage fieldwork to continue for long periods of time and in a reasonably unstructured manner, so that the regularities and rituals of everyday life can surface in a natural fashion (e.g., Van Maanen, Dabbs, & Faulkner, 1982). This approach has not been prominent in studying MIS systems but has been increasingly suggested as an attractive alternative, based on its successful use in investigating related topics (e.g., Belk, Sherry, & Wallendorf, 1988; Orlikowski, Baroudi, & Rosen, 1988).

As an initial choice, then, you should be cognizant of the significant differences between these approaches and make a clear choice between one or the other. If you select the case study approach, the remaining choices in this chapter will be relevant. If you select the ethnographic approach, you should turn elsewhere for advice (e.g., Van Maanen et al., 1982; also see Chapter 4 in this book).

BOX 9
Logical Positivism

Social science research is usually based on the collection and analysis of empirical data. Findings and conclusions are then derived from these data. *Logical positivism* is the philosophical school of thought that espouses this practice, which is the foundation for the natural sciences. Traditionally, case studies have not always been considered to be a method in the logical positivist tradition. Instead, some believe that case studies also can be done where an investigator's intuition and ideas—not reinforced by the objective collection of empirical data—have prevailed. An entirely different way of developing conclusions, apart from the scientific method, is the result (e.g., Lincoln & Guba, 1985). However, the present book, as with a prior textbook (Yin, 1984/1989), does not subscribe to such an approach. The approach here has been to base case study research within the framework of the scientific method—to develop hypotheses, collect empirical data, and develop conclusions based on the analysis of such data.

At the same time, a favoring of the case study approach over the ethnographic approach still leaves you with two basic options with regard to data collection:

1. A one-time data collection effort—typically a short number of days—for every case to be studied, in which only post-hoc longitudinal data can be collected; and

2. A more extended data collection period—typically a year or more—for each case, in which true longitudinal data can be collected.

The selection between these two types of data collection for case studies is in fact a choice in your research design. Among other factors, if the entire study is being conducted by only a single investigator, the second choice would prohibit the study from including multiple cases, unless your study were to extend over a lengthy period of time (Leonard-Barton, 1987).

DEFINING A UNIT OF ANALYSIS

As with case studies in education, the second choice is that of defining the unit of analysis, or the unit of study, for your case study. Examples of units of analyses in MIS research include the following.

- The workstation, including the machinery and individual at the workstation (e.g., studies of ergonomics)
- A local area network or an extended network (e.g., a study of electronic mail)
- The information flow within an organization (e.g., a study of the control over information within the organization)
- A collaborating set of organizations (e.g., a study of coordination among the affiliates of a holding company or the agencies in a single jurisdiction)

The unit becomes the main analytical level for the "case" being studied. A key challenge in constructing an acceptable case study research design is to ensure that the major questions of study are pertinent to the selected unit of analysis. If the questions do not coincide with the unit of analysis, the data collected may not answer them either.

At the same time, a single study may have more than one unit of analysis. A common design involves the "embedding" of units within each other (see Yin, 1984/1989, for more on this topic). For instance, a study of an entire organization (a single case study) might include a survey of workstations within the organization (embedded units of analysis) and the use of quantitative techniques to analyze the workstation data. However, as long as the major study questions remain at the organizational level, the single organization remains the major unit of analysis.

As another example, a common MIS activity is the development of new computer software. The entire software development process—a series of organizational and technical activities taking place over time—may be the unit of analysis for a case study. When the software package being developed is complicated, software teams divide the package into modules, and these modules could be one candidate for an embedded unit of analysis.

The conceptual framework for the case study might follow the software "life cycle," in which software engineers sequentially go through the following phases in developing their software packages: (a) high-level design, (b) prototyping, (c) detailed design, (d) development, (e) testing, (f) implementation, and (g) maintenance. You may want to develop hypotheses about the outcomes at each phase. For instance, a major claim of "4th-generation computer languages" is that they permit the prototyping of the final software product prior to the costly writing of computer code. Therefore, the potential software user can review these prototypes and participate at the design phase, suggesting modifications where desired. The presumed outcome is to reduce the amount of subsequent code writing and to improve the usability of the final software package.

For the individual modules within the software package, you could also trace the developmental process. For these embedded units of analysis, you might want to give closer attention to the working of the software teams and the organization of the effort, rather than the technical development of the software itself. The data from the embedded units of analysis could then provide important insights into the internal management of the software development process—possibly offering explanations for some of the outcomes related to the software package as a whole.

As shown by these examples, designating the major and embedded units of analysis is critical for identifying the relevant evidence to be collected for your case study. However, you should not make this choice in an entirely inflexible manner. Within the MIS world, for instance, the flow and control of information are becoming so important that an entire organization may be dominated by its information system. In such a situation, the traditional notion that an MIS is clearly subordinate to an organization may not be accurate, thereby rendering the identity of the relevant unit of analysis unclear. Should it be the entire organization or just the MIS system? Under such circumstances, leaving this choice open may be a desired tactic during the beginning of your study.

THE ROLE OF "THEORY"
AS PART OF DESIGN WORK

A third choice of approach to studying MISs in organizations has to do with the construction of specific theoretical propositions related to the topic of study. You should define such propositions carefully, as they represent the themes around which further design work will proceed. In fact, the identification of these theoretical issues—which will provide specific guidance and clues regarding the rest of the case study—constitutes an important step in creating the research design. In a case study of the implementation of a new MIS (Markus, 1983), for example, the simplest ingredient of a theory might be a statement such as this:

> The case study will show why implementation only succeeded when the organization was able to restructure itself, and not just overlay the new MIS on the old organizational structure. (Markus, 1983)

The statement presents, in a nutshell, a theory of MIS implementation—that is, that organizational restructuring is needed to make implementation work. An additional ingredient in the same case might be this:

The case study will also show why the simple replacement of key persons was not sufficient for successful implementation. (Markus, 1983)

This second statement represents, again in a nutshell, a *rival* theory—namely, that MIS implementation fails because of the resistance to change on the part of individual people, and that the replacement of such people is the only requirement for implementation to succeed.

As you can project, the elaboration of these two simple statements will lead to the identification of the subordinate propositions and eventually to the relevant cases to be selected and the evidence in need of being collected as part of the case study. In this sense, your complete research design embodies a "theory" of what is being studied. This theory should by no means be considered with the formality of grand theory in social science, nor are you expected to be a masterful theoretician. Rather, your goal is to have a sufficient blueprint of the theoretical issues to be studied.

An appropriately developed theory not only facilitates the data-collection phase of a case study but also reflects the level at which the generalization of the case study results will occur. This latter role of theory may be characterized as *analytic generalization*, which may be contrasted with another (and commonly confused) way of generalizing case study results known as *statistical generalization* (Yin, 1984/1989). In analytic generalization, a previously developed theory is used as a template against which to compare the empirical results of the case study. If two or more cases are shown to support the same theory, replication may be claimed. The empirical results may be considered yet more potent if two or more cases support the same theory but do not support an equally plausible, rival theory. Analytic generalization is appropriate with both single- (e.g., Allison, 1971) and multiple- (e.g., Szanton, 1981) case studies.

The contrasting, and inappropriate, manner of generalizing assumes that the selected cases are some sample of a larger universe of cases, which leads to such incorrect terminology as the "sample of cases" or the "small sample size of cases"—as if a single-case study were like a single respondent in a survey or a single subject in an experiment. Such sampling criteria will usually be irrelevant in designing case study research and should be avoided.

SUMMARY

This chapter has presented three important choices in the development of research designs for case studies of MIS systems. The development of specific research designs is strongly recommended if you are to carry out a successful case study, yet the procedure is commonly overlooked by investigators who think that doing case studies only means "getting into the field." The exercising of these three important choices is the initial and critical step in developing the specific research design.

EXERCISES

1. *Defining a management information system.* Assume you were going to do a case study of a management information system. How would you define the components the system to know what data to collect? How extensive would the system be? How far back in time would it go? What would be the basis for making these choices?

2. *Doing fieldwork in an organization.* As part of a case study of a management information system, you plan to spend time "in the field." This means visiting a specific organization and spending time with the people and systems within the organization. How would you use your time? Would you spend an entire day in the organization or only hours at a time? How would you set up any interviews in the organization—by formally scheduling them ahead of time or in informal encounters? What rationale for your routine would you give to your hosts?

3. *Studying an automated management information system.* Assume that you alone are doing a case study of a system with about 60 workstations. How much time would you spend at each workstation? Would you collect data from each one? What if more than one person can work at each workstation—would you interview all these employees? What else would you study besides the workstations?

4. *Varieties of evidence about management information systems.* Besides interviews, what other kind of evidence can or should be collected in studies of management information systems? Observational evidence? Documentary evidence?

5. *Generalizing to other cases.* Imagine that you have completed a case study of a management information system. List several possible conclusions from your study that would pertain only to the system you had just studied. Now list several possible conclusions that might be relevant to other management information systems. In what ways are these two lists different?

PART III

Evaluation

4

The Case Study Method as a Tool for Doing Evaluation

In earlier publications, I have described the usefulness of the case study method as a research tool (Yin, 1981a; 1984/1989). The purpose of this chapter is to define the method's relevance as an evaluation tool. Although the case study already has been amply promoted in this role (see Box 10), no one has attempted to explain the method's unique objectives, advantages, and procedures as an evaluation tool—compared to other methods. Therefore, you may not always understand when, how, and why you should be using case studies to conduct evaluations.

In particular, certain features of case studies have been increasingly confused with the use of (a) ethnography and (b) *grounded theory* in doing evaluations. All three are commonly intermingled under the rubric *qualitative research* in a nondiscriminatory manner (e.g., Merriam, 1988)—see Box 11. In actuality, the case study method is distinct from either of these other two qualitative methods—as well as from standard quasi-experimental (presumably quantitative) methods.

Any clarification among these methods as alternative evaluation tools, however, must be preceded by a brief definition of *evaluations*.

WHAT ARE EVALUATIONS?

Demonstration Projects as the Subject of Evaluations. For the purposes of this chapter an *evaluation* is considered a particular type of research intended to assess and explain the results of specific interventions. Many such interventions are part of *demonstration projects*—action projects or programs operated in any variety of real-life field settings.

Such demonstration projects or programs have long existed in certain fields, such as public education, and program evaluation has a long history that extends back for over 100 years (Madaus, Stufflebeam, & Scriven,

AUTHOR'S NOTE: This chapter is an expanded and adapted version of an article of the same name appearing in *Current Sociology, 40*(1), 121-137 (Spring 1992). Used by permission of Sage Publications Ltd.

BOX 10
GAO's Guidelines for Doing Case Study Evaluations

Case studies are one of the research strategies used in conducting evaluations of public programs. Investigators at the U.S. General Accounting Office (GAO) have been among the more frequent users of this strategy. To help its own evaluators, GAO published a comprehensive methodological report entitled *Case Study Evaluations* (U.S. General Accounting Office, 1987/1991). The report's usefulness and detailed operational advice make it an invaluable document for all others in the field.

The report covers three major topics—what case studies are, when they are appropriate, and what distinguishes a good case study from a not-so-good case study. Within these three topics, the report describes numerous procedures that can be followed in doing evaluations, with concrete examples from such policy areas as justice, housing, welfare, environment, education, and foreign aid. Throughout, the report emphasizes quality control and rigor—in a manner very close to Yin's original work on case study research (Yin, 1984/1989).

The report therefore freely adapts many of the procedures and concepts from Yin's earlier work—such as the use of multiple sources of evidence, the establishment of a chain of evidence, and the reliance on pattern-matching and explanation-building as the two major analytic strategies—and cites the work as a major contributing source. However, the report also augments the methodology with numerous original contributions, thereby advancing the state of the art even further.

1989). In the past three decades, the use of demonstrations in federal initiatives in the United States has received increasing attention. The role of demonstrations in federal policy-making has been a topic of extensive inquiry by such policy research organizations as The Rand Corporation (Baer, Johnson, & Merrow, 1976; Glennan et al., 1978). These investigators note that the essence of a demonstration project is that it involves "an innovation operated at or near full-scale in a realistic environment" (Glennan et al., 1978).

Based on reviews of federally funded demonstrations over the years in a broad variety of fields, the Rand team also has helped to define the purposes of demonstrations as either *policy-implementing* or *policy-formulating*. Policy-implementing demonstrations are those that take existing research ideas and put them into everyday practice. Policy-formulating demonstrations are those that produce new, field-based ideas that may then be subject to further analysis by research investigators under more controlled set-

---

BOX 11
Qualitative Research

The dichotomy between qualitative and quantitative research has become a caricature in the social sciences. Qualitative research is characterized as being "soft" social science, interested in "mushy" processes, and dealing with inadequate evidence. Quantitative research is considered hard-nosed, data-driven, outcome-oriented, and truly scientific.

This book, as with a predecessor (Yin, 1984/1989), assumes on the contrary that case study research can be qualitative *or* quantitative. The characteristics are therefore not attributes of two competing types of research. Instead, they are attributes of types of data. *Qualitative data* are data that cannot readily be converted to numerical values. Such data can be represented by categorical data, by perceptual and attitudinal dimensions not readily converted to numerical values (e.g., color perception), and by real-life events. One of the most popular ways of presenting categorical data involves "word tables," in which empirical evidence is systematically arrayed but the cells are filled with words rather than numbers.

Such a focus on qualitative (vs. quantitative) data also avoids the unproductive debate between qualitative and quantitative research. Qualitative research also can be hard-nosed, data-driven, outcome-oriented, and truly scientific. Similarly, quantitative research can be soft and mushy and deal with inadequate evidence. These are attributes of good and poor research and not of a dichotomy between two types of research (Yin, forthcoming).

---

tings. Whichever type of demonstration, the experiences are expected primarily to produce information about the implementation of a program in a real-life setting. As similarly described by two eminent social scientists (Berk & Rossi, 1990, p. 52):

> Once a prospective program has been refined through pilot studies, time comes to transport the program to a more realistic operating environment. . . . This leads to the "Can YOAA Do It?" problem: Can "your ordinary American agency" carry out the program with fidelity?

The demonstration project as a knowledge-development tool has been used in a wide range of fields, with many different types of sponsors—including state and local governments, foundations, and private industry. The demonstration may (a) target on some technological development or some social service, (b) operate in an educational or health environment, or (c) call for social change at the community level. Demonstration projects may be large or small, may involve organizations or individuals (or both), and may call for activities at multiple "sites."

Whatever its application, an intervention or a demonstration project differs from the typical "controlled" research project in two important ways. First, the traditional research project maintains tight control over experimental conditions—which may mean the testing of relatively small groups of subjects rather than widespread coverage (Howard, 1990), or an insistence on the same interventions across sites (Ginsburg, 1989). Second, the controlled research project is nearly always supervised by research-trained investigators and research-oriented organizations rather than by an operating agency, a nonprofit community organization, or a private firm (Berk & Rossi, 1990).

Evaluation as a Type of Research. Evaluations are a type of research. Like demonstration projects, evaluations also differ from controlled research projects, mainly because of the changes and uncertainties of intervening in real-life settings (Rossi & Freeman, 1993). Evaluations can therefore encounter any of the following conditions.

- Midstream changes in the intervention, thereby leading to the need for different measures of process and outcome, and possibly even the development of a new evaluation design
- Changes in participation on the part of entire "sites," thereby distorting an initial research design
- Poor retention and high attrition rates, jeopardizing any statistical analyses and therefore the evaluation results more generally
- Strained relationships between the evaluation and demonstration teams, frequently reflecting different professional incentive systems and goals (Goodstadt, 1990)

Evaluation researchers must find ways of overcoming these conditions when they occur. The researchers therefore need methodologies at their disposal to help them accomplish their objectives. In this light, let us now consider the four different methods previously mentioned—the case study method, ethnographic evaluations, grounded theory, and standard quasi-experimental evaluations.

DIFFERENCES IN ASSUMPTIONS AMONG FOUR METHODS

For the sake of argument, the four methods will be considered independently and stereotypically, to clarify their advantages and disadvantages in doing evaluations. However, in reality the four methods are not mutually exclusive and can even be used in combination in the same evaluation study. The comparative features stem from the different assumptions made by the four methods.

Case Study Evaluations. The case study method, as defined in the author's previous work (Yin, 1984/1989, p. 23), is an empirical inquiry that

investigates a contemporary phenomenon within its real-life context,
addresses a situation in which the boundaries between phenomenon and context are not clearly evident, and
uses multiple sources of evidence.

As pointed out in earlier chapters, the inclusion of the context as an integral part of the case study creates its technically distinctive characteristic: that there will always be many more variables of interest than data points to be analyzed. This technical characteristic of the case study makes statistical analysis difficult, if not irrelevant, because the data points will have no variance. However, case studies can and should still include quantitative data (numerical measurement) where relevant. In other respects, the case study is to be used as any other empirical, scientific method. The rigor of case studies should therefore be judged by the same criteria of internal validity, external validity, construct validity, and reliability.

This definition eminently suits the needs of many evaluations, for two reasons. First, the ability to incorporate an investigation of the context directly satisfies an evaluation's need to monitor and assess both the intervention and the implementation process. Second, the case study is not limited to either qualitative or quantitative data, but can incorporate both varieties of evidence.

Further, although a well-known use of the case study is to conduct an exploratory inquiry—that is, to develop new hypotheses (Ogawa & Malen, 1991; Yin, 1991)—the case study method can serve evaluation needs directly by being able to assess outcomes and to test hypotheses. To design case studies to test hypotheses, a major strategy is the prior development of theoretical formulations—of causal relationships. The strategy is even more effective if rival theories are developed, as noted in previous chapters of this book and also in Box 12. These theoretical formulations then become the main vehicle for developing generalizations from the case study findings.

For evaluations, these features of the case study method make it extremely valuable. In particular, many evaluations must go beyond assessing

---

BOX 12
Rival Theories

I have found no concept more helpful in conducting research than the concept of *rival theories*. Yet, existing texts rarely point to the importance of this concept, much less give guidance on how to develop such rivals. The most common rival theory has been the null hypothesis. A *null hypothesis* is simply the absence of the target hypothesis. In an experiment, the target hypothesis might be a significant relationship between two variables, and the null hypothesis would be the absence of this relationship (the existence of the phenomena "by chance" alone). However, for doing case studies, the best rival is not simply the absence of the target theory or hypothesis. Instead, the best rival would be a rival theory, attempting to explain the same outcome but with a different substantive theory than that of the target theory. If you have rival theories in this sense, you can collect data to test both theories and compare the results through a pattern-matching process.

The best rival also must be a true rival—one that is mutually exclusive from the target theory (for examples, see Causal Case Studies II in Chapter 1). A poor rival would be one that is substantively different from the target theory but that also can coexist with the target theory. Identifying a true rival theory is not always easy. Your best source is the existing literature on a topic: Does the literature readily separate into rival camps or theories?

---

outcomes and must test relationships between processes and outcomes. In addition, evaluations benefit greatly from any exposition of a demonstration project's "theory." Such theory is critical to understanding the innovative idea that is the subject of the demonstration; when it is ignored, those undesirable investigations are produced that fail to clarify "what is being demonstrated."

Ethnographic Evaluations. The specifications for ethnographic evaluations draw directly from existing definitions of ethnographic inquiries more generally (e.g., Fetterman, 1989; Jorgensen, 1989; Lincoln & Guba, 1985, 1986; Van Maanen, 1988; Van Maanen et al., 1982). Ethnographic evaluations are primarily guided by the assumption of multiple realities that are socially constructed—rather than the belief that there is a single, "objective" reality. For this reason, ethnographic research does not emulate the traditional paradigm of empirical science, which assumes a single objective reality that also can be repeatedly replicated. Numerous investigators have attempted to clarify the differences between the two paradigms (Guba & Lincoln, 1982; Smith & Heshusius, 1986).

As part of the assumption that there are not enduring, context-free truth statements, the ethnographic method also assumes that an investigator cannot maintain an objective distance from the phenomenon being studied. Inquiry is value-bound, not value-free. Rather than trying to create this objective distance from the topic of inquiry (i.e., through the use of "instruments"), the investigator's goal is in fact to experience directly the phenomenon being studied. Such direct experience arises from the conduct of fieldwork, with participant-observation therefore being the preferred data collection technique. Only such a technique enables the investigator to represent fairly the various multiple realities. Further, to accomplish this goal, the investigator must be free to carry out the fieldwork over long periods of time and in a reasonably unstructured manner, so that the regularities and rituals of everyday life can surface in a natural fashion (e.g., Dorr-Bremme, 1985).

In addition, ethnographic research does not necessarily begin with strong theoretical formulations. Certain theoretical tendencies emanate from the basic definition of ethnography itself—to focus on the shared beliefs, practices, artifacts, folk knowledge, and behaviors of some group of people (Goetz & LeCompte, 1984). However, theory-building rather than theory-testing is the usual objective of an ethnographic evaluation. Similarly, ethnographic evaluations value "thick" descriptions of the phenomenon being evaluated as the final outcome of study. These are lengthy and detailed renditions of the phenomenon.

The ethnographic method has been used to study different types of demonstrations, both nontechnological (Dorr-Bremme, 1985; Lincoln & Guba, 1986) and technological (Orlikowski et al., 1988; others cited in Chapter 3 of this book). For evaluations, two advocates note that the strength of the method is maximized where a strong clash in values permeates a demonstration project. Under these conditions, the evaluation has the deliberate objective of helping to define a "negotiated" set of recommendations (Lincoln & Guba, 1986).

Grounded Theory. A grounded theory "is one that is inductively derived from the study of the phenomenon it represents" (Strauss & Corbin, 1990, p. 23). Grounded theory is therefore eminently interested in theory-building, and not theory-testing. For this reason, grounded theory also incorporates the context into its investigations, because the boundaries of the phenomenon being studied may not be clear at the outset of the investigation.

Proponents of grounded theory give a basic warning in applying the method—avoid premature use of theory or prior conceptual categories

(Glaser & Strauss, 1967). Although investigators should have a good working knowledge of the previous research literature on the topic being investigated, this knowledge should not close their minds to emergent categories. The whole point of the method is to identify emergent categories from empirical data, by using qualitative data analysis methods. Such methods preclude any type of coding or enumeration that would lead to quantitative comparisons. However, the data do not have to be field-based but may even come from library sources (Glaser & Strauss, 1967, pp. 163-183).

Unlike ethnography but like case studies, grounded theory emulates the scientific method. If procedures are properly followed, "the method meets the criteria for doing 'good' science" (Strauss & Corbin, 1990, p. 27). Because of the desire to avoid premature conceptualizations, typical research questions for grounded theory may simply identify the phenomenon to be studied—for example, "How do women manage a pregnancy complicated by a chronic illness?" (Strauss & Corbin, 1990, p. 38). To go much further than specifying this question at the outset of a study would jeopardize the strengths of grounded theory, which are to develop new insights (and theory).

For evaluations, grounded theory has a certain appeal when no particular prior theory appears relevant or is explicable. However, many demonstration projects do not have the luxury of avoiding program theory or implementation theory at the outset of their projects. Yet, grounded theory may be highly relevant when the program theory is nevertheless poor and when funds may have been made available to develop such theory. Such may be the case, for instance, in demonstrations of AIDS prevention activities, where one investigator summarizing available evaluations reached the following conclusions (Rugg et al., 1990):

> There are still large gaps in our knowledge about how to intervene with high-risk and hard-to-reach individuals, let alone how to evaluate our success in doing so. (p. 89)

If a field of inquiry is in this situation, the grounded theory method might be especially helpful.

Grounded theory's specific tactics for analyzing qualitative data also are helpful in doing evaluations. Nearly every evaluation has such data, even though the evaluations also may have other types of data. For qualitative data, grounded theory's coding strategies—breaking down, conceptualizing, and reconstructing data—may therefore resolve important problems.

Quasi-Experimental Evaluations. This method has dominated the era of federal evaluations in the United States. The era largely began in the mid- to late-1960s, with the Great Society programs under Lyndon Johnson's presidency (Campbell, 1969; Rossi & Freeman, 1993). The use of control-group designs or comparisons such as time-series designs—along with heavy reliance on quantitative data collection—attempts to emulate directly the scientific method. Because quasi-experimentation may impose certain conditions over the demonstration itself—for example, in the selection of clients and the assignment of clients to different "treatment" conditions—demonstration projects wanting to use quasi-experimental evaluations often must make compromises in the design and administration of the demonstration project.

Quasi-experimental evaluations have traditionally focused on outcome assessment. Although the method is heavily oriented toward hypothesis-testing, the hypotheses focus narrowly on individual variables in the "intervention" and not necessarily on any broader theory development that may include the role of contextual conditions. Further, the method works better when individual performance (by individual clients) is the main unit of analysis rather than when organizational or technological performance is the subject of the demonstrations being evaluated. The individual unit of analysis permits the statistical analysis of individuals as members of different "groups" that have been exposed to different experimental conditions. As a way of broadening the method beyond some of its traditional uses, an alternative version of the quasi-experimental approach—"theory-driven" evaluations—has emerged in recent years (Chen, 1990).

Summary of Assumptions Among Four Methods. Table 4.1 summarizes the salient characteristics of the four methods, with regard to their basic assumptions about the nature and scope of the inquiry.

These broad contrasts among the four methods are to be compared to other works that may have obscured the differences and yielded mixed guidelines to evaluators. Patton's noted work on qualitative evaluations (1990), for instance, appears to waver among three competing conceptualizations. At one point, qualitative evaluations seem to be considered synonymous with all applied research, to be contrasted only with basic research (see pp. 11-12 of his text). At another point, the relevant characteristics of qualitative evaluations appear to be features nearly identical with ethnographic evaluation (pp. 40-41). At yet a third point, the case study is considered a type of ethnographic evaluation—in which only a

Table 4.1

Differences in Assumptions Among Four Evaluation Methods

| | Types of Evaluation | | | |
	Case Study	Ethnography	Grounded Theory	Quasi-Experiment
Design:				
1. Assumes a single objective reality that can be investigated by following the traditional rules of scientific inquiry	Yes	No	Yes	Yes
2. Can be used for theory-building	Yes	Yes	Yes	Yes
3. Also favors theory-testing	Yes	No	No	Yes
4. Considers context as essential part of phenomenon of being evaluated	Yes	Yes	Yes	No
Data Collection and Analysis:				
5. Favored data collection technique	Multiple	Participant observation	Multiple	Multiple
6. Type of data to be analyzed	Quantitative or qualitative	Mostly qualitative	Qualitative only	Mostly quantitative

single case is the subject of study (pp. 99-102). Investigators trying to design their evaluations to Patton's ideas will have difficulty in disentangling these various alternatives.

Similarly, a primer on education evaluation (Merriam, 1988) presents a "qualitative" case study approach that may call for contradictory features. Such evaluations are said at first to be discovery- and naturalistic-oriented—similar to ethnographic evaluations (pp. xii and 3). Later guidance, however, emphasizes the importance of the evaluation: (a) having a defined research problem at the outset, (b) being prepared to make deductions from theory, and (c) defining units of analyses (pp. 41-42, and 44-52)—similar to steps that would be followed in case study evaluations. Both sets of features cannot be readily incorporated into the same research design. Further, the text is not clear whether a qualitative case study can only be descriptive (pp. 6-7) or whether it also can be explanatory (p. 28).

To show why there are indeed operational differences among these four methods, the next section reviews specific evaluation techniques.

DIFFERENCES AMONG FOUR METHODS IN DESIGNING AND CONDUCTING EVALUATIONS

The contrasting techniques favored by the four methods are a direct result of the different assumptions made by the four methods, as highlighted in Table 4.1. For brevity's sake, the discussion of these differences and techniques is divided into three broad phases in designing and conducting evaluations: initial design, data collection and analysis, and evaluation reporting and utilization.

Initial Design. For the four methods, the initial design for an evaluation is heavily influenced by the method's orientation to the roles of theory and of context.

As previously noted, case study designs are embedded in both. For evaluation purposes, explanatory rather than merely descriptive case studies are desired. The case study design should be preceded by thorough preparation, including the following.

- Reviewing the literature
- Accumulating all evidence related to the goals and design of the program being evaluated, including interviews of program officials, their sponsors, and other "stakeholders"
- Developing specific hypotheses about the program being evaluated, by constructing a "program logic model" (Wholey, 1979)
- Developing taxonomies or other schemes for understanding the context within which the program operates
- Defining key design components—for example, the units of analysis and embedded units of analysis, if any

This preparation would help the ensuing evaluation deal with at least three important issues not always addressed by the other methods. First, in defining the *case* or main unit of analysis, the case study investigator(s) would have to consider explicitly the appropriate definition of the *program* and therefore the intervention being evaluated (see Chapter 5). This definition is often taken for granted, or follows artifactual realities such as administrative criteria.

BOX 13
Program Logic Models

Every public program—in schools, economic development, health care, criminal justice, housing, and so on—may be considered an *intervention*. As interventions, every program is therefore intended to produce a different set of outcomes than would have existed in the absence of the program. How a program is to produce the desired outcomes, in theoretical terms, may be reflected by its program logic model. If the theory makes sense, an evaluation may then be conducted to test the theory by collecting actual data and determining whether the theory appears to work or not.

The model is conceptual, arguing a series of cause-and-effect relationships —with events occurring over time—between the program and its desired outcomes. The establishment of the program logic model is itself a design and analytic activity (Wholey, 1979). The logic model typically attempts to connect a program's resources to its activities—and its activities in turn to immediate outcomes and ultimate outcomes.

Sometimes, the program is discovered to be illogically related to its outcomes, in which case no evaluation will be feasible, either. The establishment of a compelling logic model is therefore essential in two respects. First, program operators should have a defensible model before they implement their programs. Second, program evaluators should determine that a logical model is in place before proceeding with the remainder of an evaluation.

Second, the case study evaluation will produce explicit theorizing about the context. For example, such theorizing may take the form of prototypic typologies of program *sites* and ultimately the development of the needed replication rationale if the program has multiple sites and therefore warrants a multiple-case study design (Yin, 1984/1989, pp. 52-58). (Such a replication rationale can be based on either contextual or programmatic variations.)

Third, whether a single- or multiple-case design, this theorizing also calls for the explicit development of potential (and even rival) program logic models, which are hypothesized causal flows to explain how a program is to operate successfully (see Box 13). These models need to discriminate between *program* theories and *implementation* theories (Bickman, 1987). For example, in a math/science program, the program theory could link the opportunity to take Algebra II with all subsequent advancement in math, engineering, or science. In contrast, the implementation theory might call attention to the need for a capable project director, sufficient resources to conduct the program, and other administrative conditions.

Many evaluation designs fail to discriminate properly between these two types of theories. Although substantive advances in knowledge depend heavily on the testing of program theories, the ensuing evaluation may lead only to additional knowledge about implementation processes. Such processes are important but are not a substitute for learning about the substantive topic—namely, math and science education.

Figure 4.1 shows another example of working with program theories. This particular model is not about any single program, but covers the variety of interventions possible when trying to ameliorate an increasingly difficult contemporary problem: drug-trafficking and criminal behavior by members of youth gangs. Each circled number in Figure 4.1 illustrates a potentially different intervention. Depending on the intervention, different evaluation designs would be relevant. The figure is helpful because it places all the major gang-related interventions within the same framework.

None of the other three methods would necessarily follow the same procedures at the design stage of an evaluation. Ethnographic evaluations do, in fact, also treat the definition of a program and its boundaries as problematic (Dorr-Bremme, 1985), and would be concerned with the context. However, ethnographic evaluations would not necessarily favor such intense, a priori development of theoretical propositions, program models, and hypotheses to be tested. Similarly, grounded theory would strongly discourage a theory-testing posture. Finally, quasi-experimental evaluations are committed primarily to the development of designs that permit the comparison and interpretation of outcomes—in the presence or absence of a "treatment." Only secondarily would such evaluations be concerned with the identification of program theory and the hypothesis-testing of causal flows—and even if the evaluation were augmented in this manner, coverage of contextual conditions would be highly limited.

Data Collection and Analysis. Each method's favored data collection and analysis techniques also reflect the method's initial orientation and its assumptions about whether to follow the rules of traditional scientific inquiry.

The initial case study orientation is toward multiple sources of evidence. The case study evaluation can therefore include the use of document analysis, open- and closed-ended interviews, quantitative analysis of archival data, and direct field observations. The multiple sources are intended to be used in a converging fashion, so that data should triangulate over the "facts" of a case—see Box 14. Quantitative and qualitative data are both considered potentially important and relevant. Fieldwork techniques are usually—but not always—part of the repertoire.

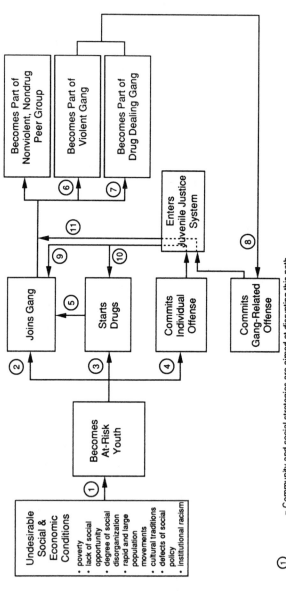

Figure 4.1. Illustrative Analytic Framework for Gang-Related Drug Prevention

---

BOX 14
Triangulation

Every student knows the original derivation of the concept of *triangulation*: a point in geometric space may be definitively established by specifying the intersection of three vectors (not two or one; further, four would be redundant). This concept has been borrowed for dealing with social science evidence: The most robust fact may be considered to have been established if three (or more) sources all coincide.

Consider the difficulty of establishing the occurrence of an event. You would be more confident in saying that the event actually had occurred if your study showed that information from interviews, documents, and your own observations all pointed in the same direction. With such converging evidence, you might even feel very confident about your conclusion that the event had occurred. This type of triangulation is the most desired pattern for dealing with case study data, and you should always seek to attain such an outcome. An important clue is to ask the same question of different sources of evidence; if all sources point to the same answer, you have successfully triangulated your data.

This orientation toward data collection, along with the initial causal design, enables a case study evaluation to cover both the processes and outcomes of the program being evaluated. The process component of the evaluation should not be considered an end in itself but should be linked through the hypothesized program model to the full variety of relevant outcomes. At the same time, the process information may be reported early in the life cycle of the evaluation, if needed, to provide formative feedback (Scriven, 1967) to program managers.

The case study's acceptance of the rules of traditional scientific inquiry means that the data collection should be done with explicitly developed protocols, instruments, and other tools external to the investigator. Development of these data collection instruments may take considerable time and effort. Further, investigators may have to be trained to use these instruments properly, and pilot testing and other preliminary empirical work can and should focus on checks for reliability and construct validity.

For data analysis, one of but several strategies for the case study evaluation is pattern-matching (Campbell, 1975; Yin, 1984/1989). The pattern-matching can be between theorized and observed variables, whether process or outcome variables. If outcome variables are involved, the pattern-matching is not too different from one of the quasi-experimental designs and in this respect overlaps with this approach: the nonequivalent dependent variables design (Cook & Campbell, 1979, p. 118). Also, the pattern-matching strategy is especially potent if comparisons are made between two or more rival, hypothesized processes or outcomes and the observed processes or outcomes.

By comparison, data collection for ethnographic evaluation is heavily influenced by the method's assumptions regarding multiple realities and the rejection of the rules of traditional scientific inquiry. The method regards the investigator—and not some mechanical tool or instrument—as the primary instrument of data collection. As a result, the investigator must engage in fieldwork, favoring such techniques as participant-observation. Data collection is to be naturalistic, to favor process over outcomes, and to be intensely descriptive, leading ultimately to a rich, "thick" description of the program being evaluated (Van Maanen, 1988). In contrast to grounded theory, the relevant data can include quantitative and not merely qualitative information, and data analysis techniques can include the quantitative assessment of qualitative data (Johnson, 1978).

Both grounded theory and quasi-experimental evaluations emulate the rules of traditional scientific inquiry. These methods are therefore concerned with instrumentation, reliability, and validity. However, by definition, grounded theory limits itself to qualitative data and avoids quantitative data. To this extent, the favored data collection techniques evolve around the collection and analysis of categorical data, which—in comparison to ethnographic evaluation—may or may not be field-based. Conversely, quasi-experimental evaluations tend to favor quantitative rather than qualitative data. Where qualitative data are used, the evaluations quickly convert such data into quantifiable form, using techniques that have become well developed and increasingly potent over the past two decades (for a solid, earlier text, see Goodman, 1978)—a step, however, that grounded theory would clearly avoid.

Evaluation Reporting and Utilization. Differences among the four methods are also clearly evident in this third phase of designing and conducting evaluations.

In the past, the case study evaluation report has been one of the weakest aspects of the case study method. The weakness stemmed from the frequent failure to create a case study database apart from the case study report (Yin, 1984/1989, pp. 98-102). As a result, the narrative portion of the case study report was difficult to interpret: Was it the evidence for the case study, or was it the investigator's interpretation of the evidence? Was the case study underdocumented and overconcluded? This confusion possibly accounts for one of the traditional criticisms of case study evaluations—their alleged subjectivity (e.g., House, 1982).

The desired remedy has two steps. First, the data collection process should culminate in the creation of a formal, case study database—whether including organized field notes, archival documents and records in retrievable form, tabular materials, or even the investigator's own narrative responses to the case study protocol. The ultimate case study report needs to be completely separate from this database. In theory, an external observer should be able to inspect the database whether or not a report exists.

Second, the report should contain formal presentations of the relevant evidence and data from the database—so that the reader can observe, question, and re-interpret (if necessary) the data independent of any reading of the report's narrative portion. The presentation of the data may take the form of numeric tables, word tables, vignettes, reproduced documents, or other materials that also may appear in a separate appendix. Whatever the form, the narrative of the case study report should relate specific interpretations and conclusions to specific data presentations in the report.

The achievement of these two steps is minimally necessary to produce a high-quality case study evaluation report. In turn, this achievement will increase the rigor of the case study evaluation (e.g., Yin, 1984/1989) and increase the potential for utilizing the results (e.g., Alkin et al., 1979).

The case study approach also has certain other characteristics that favor increased utilization of the evaluation results. Because the explanatory case study has focused on process and not just outcome variables, the astute case study evaluator may have developed insights into the program's design and implementation. This information is frequently valuable to program officials, whether provided in a formative or summative mode (Scriven, 1967). Further, because the case study design has emphasized the development of a program logic model—hypothesizing causal links between process and outcome variables—a case study evaluation also may develop important explanatory information of interest to officials. Such utility of explanatory case studies has been reported in research on business firms (Gummesson, 1988, p. 76). In either case, the likelihood of evaluation utilization will be increased.

By comparison again, the other three methods will differ from the case study evaluation. The ethnographic report will emphasize "thick" (detailed) description and will consist largely of descriptive, narrative text. The importance of this narrative in ethnographic research has led investigators to examine explicitly the strategies for developing a narrative's analytic structure and quality (e.g., Van Maanen, 1988). Utilization of ethnographic evaluation may be difficult, however, for two reasons. The narrative will be extensive and possibly tedious to read. Also, the ethnographic evaluation may not have focused on process-outcome linkages or even on outcomes at all.

The grounded theory report and the utilization of its findings will vary. In some instances, the report may be similar to that of an ethnographic evaluation, and the utilization experience may encounter barriers similar to those of ethnographic evaluations. In other instances, the report may focus on the discovery and development of certain new concepts, and may assume a written or verbal form (Strauss & Corbin, 1990, p. 20). Utilization of the results then may be high.

Quasi-experimental evaluation reports also vary, although their key ingredient is to have clearly presented quantitative evidence. Some reports have so much evidence that the pertinent conclusions are difficult to find, leading to lower levels of utilization. Other reports will be highly useful because they will have made a clear assessment of program outcomes, even if no attempt was made to explain these outcomes. However, this type of summative knowledge—"the program worked or it did not work"— may not involve explanations of why the outcomes occurred, and the type of utilization may simply be a "go-no-go" decision about the program that had been evaluated.

Overall, the quasi-experimental evaluation may not experience much utilization compared to the other three methods—case study, ethnography, and grounded theory—because the quasi-experimental design may not have focused on any process variables. The evaluator would then have few insights into program operations or implementation to offer, in comparison to the other three methods. At the same time, some quasi-experimental evaluators do not consider utilization to be an important objective in the first place (Berk & Rossi, 1990).

SUMMARY OF STEPS IN DESIGNING AND CONDUCTING CASE STUDY EVALUATIONS

The preceding sections have provided information on the major contrasts among four evaluation methods. Given this understanding, the following section summarizes the major steps in doing case study evaluations.

1. Develop a Hypothesized Understanding of the Program Being Evaluated. You must base your initial design of a case study evaluation on a thorough understanding of a program's intended operations and outcomes, with explicit attention to contextual conditions. This should be a hypothesized understanding of the program, open to further corroboration and revision. All basic concepts—such as the definition of the program itself —should be considered open for later modification. Your understanding of the program should be reflected in at least two ways: a program logic model tracing the causal flows of the program, and an emerging taxonomy of contextual conditions within which the program operates.

2. *Immerse This Understanding Within Previous Research, Wherever Possible.* You should place this hypothesized understanding of the program within a broader range of theory and practice, as reflected by previous research. Wherever possible, *rival* theories and hypotheses should be identified. Such embedding of the program's theory within this broader range will lead to three invaluable benefits. First, the hypothesized understanding of the program may be clarified even further. Second, the rival theories or hypotheses will lead to potent strategies for analyzing the data. Third, the broader range of theory and practice will be the main vehicle for generalizing the results of the evaluation.

3. *Tentatively Define the Main and Subordinate Units of Analysis.* The program itself will usually be the main unit of analysis. For many federal programs that in turn support efforts at multiple individual sites, the federal program is likely to be the main unit of analysis, but embedded units might be the multiple individual sites and even the clients at each site (see Chapter 3). However, in this example, the essence of the case study method is in dealing with the main unit of analysis—the federal program—for which $N = 1$.

This step also includes the tentative definition of a replication design, if multiple-cases are to be evaluated. The replication can occur with the main unit of analysis (a comparison of two federal programs) or with subordinate units of analysis.

As your case study progresses, the initial understanding of the program as well as these units of analyses may turn out to have been incorrect or imprecise. You are encouraged to make revisions in the research design— but for any major revision, you may have to start instrumentation and data collection afresh. (One tactic would be to redefine the prior data collection as a pilot phase for the new design and data collection.) Failure to start afresh—a common problem in doing case studies—will seriously jeopardize the presumed objectivity and quality of your final evaluation.

4. Establish a Schedule and Procedure for Making Interim and Final Reports. A valuable characteristic of the case study evaluation is its ability to provide feedback throughout the life cycle of the evaluation. You should maximize this capability by developing clear schedules and procedures, with program and sponsoring officials, for this feedback. In some situations, formal briefings may be the desired process. In other situations, the program officials may form a "workgroup" that communicates on an intermittent basis with you and your study team.

5. Define and Test Instruments, Protocols, and Field Procedures. You will usually need different instruments and procedures for each unit of analysis. Further, your case study evaluation can use any relevant data collection procedure, including fieldwork and participant-observation, surveys, quantitative modeling of archival data, and methods of document analysis derived from the field of history.

The variables and categories of data to be collected should reflect your hypothesized understanding of the program and the rival theories or hypotheses previously defined. However, the data collection plans and procedures cannot be made final until you have done some pilot testing, including a thorough determination of the types of evidence likely to be available for the evaluation.

6. Collect, Analyze, and Synthesize Data. In case study work, data collection and analysis are likely to occur in an intermingled fashion. This is because the sources of evidence are likely to vary from site to site or from case to case. In this situation, you must perform more like a detective than a research assistant—evaluating the adequacy of evidence as it is being collected. Thus case study investigators must be seasoned investigators who (a) understand the objectives of the inquiry and can identify relevant evidence even though specific sources may vary and (b) document thoroughly the methodological steps taken to assure an unbiased data collection process despite this variation.

7. Create a Case Study Database. When data collection has been completed, you must create a formal database or archive, covering the whole range of quantitative and qualitative data that were collected. You should organize this archive systematically, to permit efficient access for analytic and reporting purposes.

8. Analyze the Evidence. Depending on the type of evidence collected, your case study evaluation can include a broad array of analytic techniques. For instance, the same evaluation could include highly quantitative analyses of individual client outcomes and pattern-matching analyses of organizational and implementation processes. You should be aware that the analysis process can lead to the need for additional data collection, which might then be undertaken—but again with the proper methodological cautions. In some evaluation studies, data collection may have been deliberately designed to occur at multiple points in time, over an extended period of time.

9. Compose the Case Study Report. Your report may take a variety of forms, but the essential characteristics are that the report (a) is separate from your case study database and (b) contains explicit presentations of the key evidence used to draw your conclusions.

CONCLUSION: THE CASE STUDY METHOD AS A DISTINCTIVE EVALUATION TOOL

This chapter has summarized the case study method as a distinctive evaluation tool. Such distinctiveness is reflected by contrasting the method with other evaluation tools—ethnographic evaluations, grounded theory, and quasi-experimental evaluations—as well as by enumerating the specific procedures to be followed in a case study evaluation. The major claim is that the case study method is a valuable evaluation method, distinctive in its ability to do the following.

- Attend to program operation and context
- Accommodate single programs (cases) or situations with small numbers of cases
- Capture process and outcomes in a causal logic model and thereby provide useful and intermittent feedback to program officials
- Adapt to the availability of different types of evidence
- Assess outcomes and test causal theories and rival theories
- Develop lessons generalizable to the major substantive themes in a field

As a final reminder, even though the case study is a distinctive evaluation method, it can be used in combination with the other methods. The purpose of the present chapter has been to highlight the differences among these methods for the sake of making comparisons. However, the methods are compatible and complementary, as long as their features are not mixed within the same design.

One desired pattern is to have a single evaluation consist of multiple substudies, with each substudy having its own research design and data collection techniques. In this way, one of the substudies might be a case study, and another might be an ethnography. If the program being evaluated is sufficiently complicated, you might find this use of multiple methods to be a very attractive strategy.

EXERCISES

1. *Defining a demonstration project.* What are demonstration projects, and what is their purpose? Identify a demonstration project (if you are not familiar with one, select one from the policy research literature). If the project is successful, what would it have "demonstrated"?

2. *Defining a program logic model.* Every demonstration project should have an underlying theory—explaining how and why certain activities (an "intervention") will lead to the outcomes of the demonstration. Define this program logic model, either for the specific demonstration project you have selected for Question 1 above or for some other demonstration project.

3. *Distinguishing "program" from "implementation" theories.* To what extent did your preceding program logic model reflect programmatic events? Implementation events? Which components of your program logic model are truly only applicable to the chosen demonstration project, and which components might actually be applicable to nearly all other demonstrations? Can you explain the differences between these two types of components?

4. *Comparing three types of methods.* Using your own terms, describe the main differences between the case study method, ethnography, and grounded theory. Why are the three methods, regardless of their differences, all commonly (but, incorrectly) considered as qualitative methods?

5. *Reporting the results of case study evaluations.* What are two ways of increasing the quality of case study evaluation reports? How can you increase the likely utilization of the reports? Do "thick" descriptions of the program being evaluated help quality? Utilization?

5

Case Study Designs for Evaluating High-Risk Youth Programs: The Program Dictates the Design

WHEN CASE STUDY DESIGNS MAY BE NEEDED

Evaluations concern the assessing of outcomes and the making of causal inferences to explain these outcomes. These scientific objectives are facilitated by the use of research designs.

Effective research designs assure that (a) empirical results are interpretable with minimum ambiguity and (b) interpretation will bear directly on the causal hypothesis of study. The well-articulated design therefore serves as a technical or logical plan, guiding data collection and analysis to achieve these two goals. Without such designs, the results of empirical studies may be uninterpretable, regardless of the precision of the instruments or measures used. For behavioral research, at least three types of designs appear to be needed, to cover different real-life situations.

Experimental Designs. The first is the classic experimental research design, rooted in early work in educational research (McCall, 1923, cited in Campbell & Stanley, 1963) and in agricultural research (Fisher, 1935). To use this class of designs, a study must meet four requirements:

1. Have a unit of analysis with a sufficient number of "subjects" to produce multiple data points for any given variable;
2. Have a limited number of variables of interest—usually much smaller than the number of data points available;
3. Have the experimenter's ability to control and manipulate the variables of interest; and
4. Have random assignment of subjects to the treatment and control conditions.

AUTHOR'S NOTE: This chapter was originally presented at the International Workshop on Evaluating Intervention Strategies, cosponsored by the Organization for Economic Cooperation and Development, the U.S. Department of Education, and the U.S. Department of Health and Human Services, Washington, DC, May 1991.

Studies that meet these four requirements can use numerous research designs, which have been well documented in psychology (e.g., Sidowski, 1966) and the other social sciences (e.g., Kidder et al., 1986).

Quasi-Experimental Designs. If a study cannot meet requirement 3 or 4, another type of research design becomes relevant—quasi-experimental designs (see also Chapter 4). The development of such designs has followed Campbell and Stanley's (1963) seminal work. Thus quasi-experimental designs are used when the investigator cannot control or manipulate variables and cannot assure that "subjects" are assigned to particular "treatment" conditions. The loss of such control generally occurs when a study takes place in a real-life setting rather than in an experimental laboratory—a characteristic explicitly recognized in the subtitle (*Design and Analysis Issues for Field Settings*) of Cook and Campbell's widely used text on quasi-experimental designs (1979).

Case Study Designs. Until recently, these first two types of research designs attracted nearly all the methodological attention. Yet, another situation arises when a study cannot meet the first, and not just the third, of the preceding requirements. Technically, the situation coincides directly with the technical characteristic of case studies—that the number of "subjects" or data points is so small that it cannot outnumber the variables of interest (requirements 1 and 2), as well as when the investigator also cannot control or manipulate the relevant variables (requirements 3 and 4). As a result, such techniques as "grouping subjects" or "measuring the variance among a set of data points"—critical to both experimental and quasi-experimental designs—cannot be used.

By definition, the case study is accustomed to dealing with this situation. A case study calls for intensive amounts of data (i.e., a large number of variables) about a small number or a single unit of analysis (the "case"). Investigators use this method because certain topics of inquiry are so complex that the phenomenon of interest is not readily distinguishable from its contextual conditions, and data are therefore needed about both. Studies done in this fashion cannot readily use experimental or quasi-experimental designs. Case study designs may instead be needed. Figure 5.1 compares the three situations.

Methodological research has not yet uncovered the full variety or taxonomy of case study designs. The state of knowledge about these designs—compared to knowledge about experimental and quasi-experimental designs—is more primitive and limited. However, two important characteristics

| | Type of Design | | |
Situation	Experimental	Quasi-Experimental	Case Study
Sufficient number of "subjects" producing multiple data points	■	■	
Limited number of variables of interest (fewer than the data points)	■	■	
Experimenter's ability to control and manipulate the variables of interest	■		

Figure 5.1. Summary of Situations Requiring Possibly Different Designs

of these designs are known at this time (Yin, 1984/1989). First, there are at least two subtypes of case study designs—single-case designs and multiple-case designs—and the appropriate multiple-case designs must follow a replication rather than sampling logic. The cross-case replication logic is in fact parallel to a "cross-experiment" logic. Following this logic, case studies may be deliberately selected, post hoc, to replicate the same or different (intervention) conditions and therefore to approximate the conditions of the third requirement above, even though the investigator has not manipulated these conditions directly. Of course, a measure of luck and fortunate circumstance are needed to find such replication candidates, and this does not always happen. When no other cases are available for replication, the investigator is limited to single-case study designs.

Second, generalization of the results from either type of case study design is made to theory, and not to "populations." In other words, the correct case study design identifies a theory that a case study is trying to test, rather than regarding individual case studies as data points or part of a sample. Figure 5.2 labels these as "Level Two" inferences and suggests that case studies do not have the "Level One" inferences of experiments (and quasi-experiments) and surveys. The theorized pattern of results is then pattern-matched against the empirically observed data from the case study. Multiple cases, if available, strengthen these results by replicating the pattern-matching and yielding greater confidence in the robustness of the theory. Combined, these two essential characteristics help assure that case study research can lead to cumulative scientific knowledge, with specific cases designed so that they can "test" and advance theory.

80

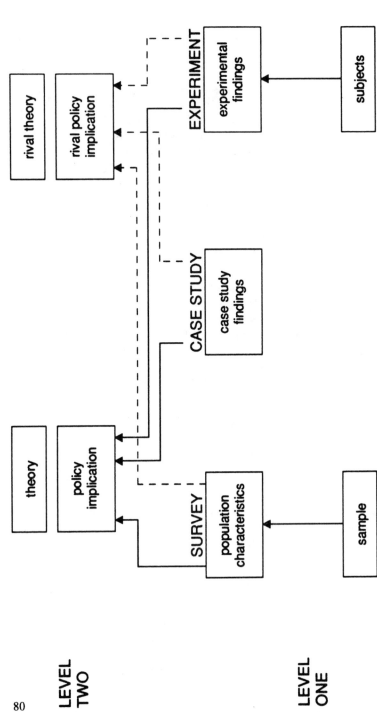

Figure 5.2. Making Inferences: Two Levels
Source: Yin, 1984/1989.

The purpose of this chapter is to illustrate potential case study designs as they might be applied to evaluating high-risk youth programs (also see Chapter 6). Such programs aim at intervening with youths and young children to increase the likelihood of their academic success and ultimately their occupational and social integration as adults. The programs may take varied forms, operating in school and out-of-school settings. In addition, the programs may not only focus on educational objectives but also can address social conditions such as substance abuse prevention.

CASE STUDY DESIGNS APPLIED TO HIGH-RISK YOUTH PROGRAMS

Preconditions Leading to the Use of Case Studies. On the surface, the evaluation of high-risk youth programs, as with many other topics of inquiry, can be addressed by any of the three types of designs just discussed: experiments, quasi-experiments, and case studies. The choice depends first on your ability to manipulate the variables of interest and second on the number of data points available. The latter depend heavily on the questions of study.

To use an experimental design, you would have to be able to assign individual youth to different "treatment conditions"—where the presentation of the relevant variables would be manipulable. Quasi-experimental designs would have to be used if individual youth could not be assigned to these conditions and the relevant variables could not be manipulated. However, case study designs would be needed if the study questions led to the creation of more variables than data points—and the relevant variables also could not be manipulated.

For example, the classic case study might be applied to an individual youth. The single youth would be the subject of intensive data collection, possibly because of the desire to understand the youth's peer, family, and community relationships. In other words, this study would have been driven by a desire to understand the contextual conditions of the youth's world, thereby creating a very large number of variables of study even though only a single youth (or single data point) was the subject of study. Even if you studied two, three, or a handful of youths in a similar manner, the context would be so rich that the number of variables would always far exceed the number of data points. In other words, the degrees of freedom would always be insufficient compared to the number of variables (see Box 15), thereby making most behavioral statistics irrelevant.

BOX 15
Degrees of Freedom

The single-case study has long been associated with the availability of a single degree of freedom (Campbell, 1975). From a statistical viewpoint, the fewer degrees of freedom, the larger any differences among (treatment and control) values must be, to attain statistically significant results. Because the case study has been associated with a single degree of freedom, the results must be very strong. Although case study analysis, as depicted in this book, does not follow traditional statistical testing procedures (such tests reflect the desire to generalize from a sample to a population—which should *not* be a goal of doing case studies), the concept of having low degrees of freedom is nevertheless very useful. If doing case studies, you should strive for strong, starkly contrasting results. Without such dramatic results, your conclusions are likely to be successfully challenged.

At the same time, the evaluation of high-risk youth programs need not be limited to individual youths as a unit of analysis. Several other potential units also are relevant, and for each unit, the pertinent study questions may include complex contextual conditions—such as the political environment, social change conditions, and organizational efforts. What other units of analysis might be relevant than the individual youth? At least four such units are possible, and in different situations all have been considered high-risk youth "programs":

1. an individual *project* devoted to high-risk youth,
2. an *organization* operating several projects devoted to high-risk youth,
3. a nationally sponsored *program*, consisting of many funded projects, and
4. a *national effort* devoted to the educational needs of high-risk youth.

Note that these units would not be distinctive if they were merely defined as aggregates of individual youths. For instance, a study question for a high-risk youth program might simply be the extent to which the youth in the program benefited. For this and related study questions, the effective unit of analysis would still be the individual youth (and the pertinent design might still be an experimental or quasi-experimental design). In contrast, an alternative study question could be the extent to which the program used or created new ideas about high-risk youth interventions. Now the effective unit of analysis would be the program itself, and case study designs might be more relevant than either experimental or quasi-experimental designs.

The preceding example shows how study questions lead to the selection of the appropriate method—experiments, quasi-experiments, or case studies—as the desired evaluation method. However, such selection is only the first of many critical steps leading to a final evaluation design. If case studies are the choice, equally important is the recognition that (a) different study questions lead to concentration on (b) different units of analysis, in turn leading to (c) different case study designs. Illustrations for each possible unit of analysis—besides the individual youth as a unit of analysis just described—follow.

Project-Based Designs. In evaluating high-risk youth projects, data about youth interventions and performance may be only one facet of the complete evaluation. Your evaluation might also collect and analyze data about the project as a whole—in which case only a single data point would be available, even though many variables were of interest. Even if multiple projects were the target of the evaluation, the number of projects (and hence data points) would only rarely exceed the number of variables of interest.

Take the following example of a high-risk youth project. The example draws from a real-life project operated in Florida, initiated in 1988 (Yin, Schiller, & Teitelbaum, 1991). The project focused on reducing the social dysfunction of adolescent mothers who had been cocaine users during their pregnancies—and of their drug-exposed babies and toddlers. The major goal of the project was to disrupt the known intergenerational aspects of substance abuse—a phenomenon that has produced children of substance abusers (COSAs) as a major category of high-risk youth. The project's activities included training classes for the mothers, intensive case management for them and their offspring, and day-care and child development services for the offspring during the mothers' working hours. Because of the advanced, state-of-the-art nature of this project, only a handful of mothers and their offspring were included in the project's initial operation.

This real-life sample project was therefore complex in several respects. First, the "youth" represented an embedded unit of analysis within the major unit of the project itself. Second, this embedded unit had a "dual" nature—the youthful adolescent mothers as well as their offspring who could themselves become high-risk youth in their later years. Third, the project consisted of a multifaceted intervention, dealing with the following areas.

- The mother's training as a parent
- The development of the mother's support group
- The infant's or toddler's health

Fourth, the evaluation questions were not limited to either of the embedded units of analysis but also dealt with the project as a whole—Had it implemented a state-of-the-art practice, and Was it a success? The appropriate single-case study design would therefore begin with two steps: the identification of project-based outcomes, and the development of project-based theories to account for these outcomes.

Organization-Based Designs. As an alternative to individual projects, your evaluation might be trying to assess the development and success of organizations that operate high-risk youth projects. Such evaluations recognize that individual projects may be unstable over time, and that broader organizational capabilities may be needed to initiate and sustain such projects. The desired study might want to investigate how these organizations operate, and how they sustain effective projects on an ongoing basis. In this situation, the organization would be the appropriate unit of analysis for developing a case study design.

In the high-risk field, an illustrative organization was the subject of a recent case study (Yin, Schiller, & Teitelbaum, 1991). The organization had been founded in 1970 and operated several dozen projects, of which the COSA project just described was but one. The organization aimed at providing a "continuum of services" for at-risk individuals, so that it could deal with the "whole youth." In particular, the organization had developed a broad array of projects dealing with at-risk youths in the context of their immediate families or significant others, not just in isolation (as in traditional school-based programs). In 20 years, the organization had succeeded in growing to a size of $11 million in annual operations, with a staff of over 275 employees and a client base of about 50,000 persons. Further, the organization had successfully started and sustained innovative projects and achieved a national reputation for its work.

The design of an evaluation of this organization would begin with the identification of organization-based outcomes. The design would continue with the development of theories and rival theories accounting for such outcomes. In the illustrative case, the hypothesized conditions leading to success included the following.

- An ability to deal with multiple sources of financial support—of critical importance in the high-risk field because of the presence of multiple support agencies
- The explicit development of extended career paths for individual staff, to reduce staff burnout and turnover
- Maintenance of strong ties with the local community, assuring the initiation of high-priority projects that would receive community support and cooperation

In a multiple-case study, establishing the presence of these conditions in other organizations would be a major replication objective.

Program-Based Designs. Yet a third evaluation might focus on a nationally sponsored high-risk program. Such a program typically involves the awarding of many individual projects. Nevertheless, the program might still have a singular mission—usually found in a legislative or policy mandate. Assessing the achievement of these program objectives would go beyond the evaluation of the individual projects. In the evaluation field, focusing on a single program of this sort has been the most common activity falling within the definition of a *program evaluation.* A potential evaluation design for this unit of analysis is therefore reviewed in greater detail than the other units of analysis.

An illustrative but existing high-risk youth program is one supported by the U.S. Department of Health and Human Services (HHS). This "high-risk youth program," administered by HHS's Office for Substance Abuse Prevention, was created by anti-drug-abuse legislation passed in 1987 and amended in 1989. The programmatic goal has been to sponsor demonstration projects, which implement new practices for preventing substance abuse among high-risk youth in real-life settings. During the past three years, the program has invested about $55 million in making over 300 awards to local sites to operate such projects.

This demonstration program is typical of many federal initiatives. The program aims to improve the state of the practice by successfully field-testing new ideas about new practices. Implementation success should be replicated at multiple sites, and the new ideas should then be disseminated to and eventually incorporated into permanent service settings across the country. Demonstration programs are therefore different from two other common types of federal programs: research programs and block grant (service) programs. Figure 5.3 depicts these differences, suggesting that research programs largely operate in nonfield settings and that block grants are intended to support service delivery directly. In contrast, demonstration programs are intended to take laboratory-based ideas and test them in the field, thereby leading to new (and more effective) designs for service delivery systems. (The demonstrations also may discover new, field-based ideas, which would then be fed back to research for further testing and validation.)

The evaluation design for a high-risk youth program would follow the same procedures as previously indicated for individual projects or organizations: the identification of pertinent outcomes and then of hypothesized

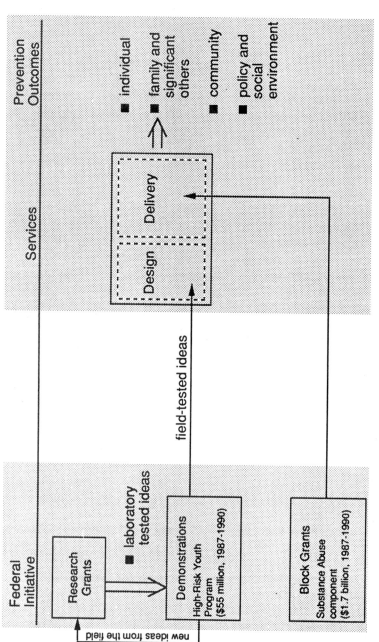

Figure 5.3. High-Risk Youth Program

theories to account for these outcomes. However, the substance of the evaluation—testing a demonstration theory—would be entirely different from those of project or organization evaluations. Figure 5.4 shows how a design might be started. The figure shows an illustrative study question, the relevant outcomes for a demonstration program (as opposed to a block grant or service program), and the hypothesized process whereby these outcomes are produced.

The ensuing study would be a complex case study, to test this demonstration theory. Information would be collected about the program as a whole, about the collection of funded projects, and even about youth outcomes within these projects. For instance, an important part of the theory would be that field projects had been successfully implemented, with success defined by the four bulleted items shown in Figure 5.4—including effective outcomes at the project level. Nevertheless, the main outcomes of interest for this case study would still be those reflecting the programmatic demonstration theory, not individual or project goals.

Not shown in Figure 5.4 is any rival theory. A hypothetical rival would be that the existing ideas to be drawn from R&D were sufficiently operational that further field-testing was not necessary. Such a rival would claim that the most important ideas were already being transferred directly from R&D into service practices, bypassing the entire demonstration cycle. Any findings in support of this rival would severely undermine the initially stated demonstration theory. Thus the ensuing case study would be designed to collect sufficient information to test this rival along with the main demonstration theory.

Note how the theory and rival theory for studying this single high-risk demonstration program differ markedly from the preceding theories for high-risk projects or organizations. Further, the articulation of the theory suggests that other cases might in fact be available for replication purposes, even though there was only one high-risk youth program: Because the theory deals with demonstration programs, a demonstration program in a related field could serve as a candidate for replication and further testing—of the demonstration theory and its rival.

Designs for Evaluating National Efforts. Finally, a fourth evaluation study might focus on the degree of success of national efforts to deal with high-risk youths. In the United States, such an evaluation might begin with the observations that high-risk conditions are directly related to race and ethnicity (Hodgkinson, 1989; *Kids Count Data Book,* 1991):

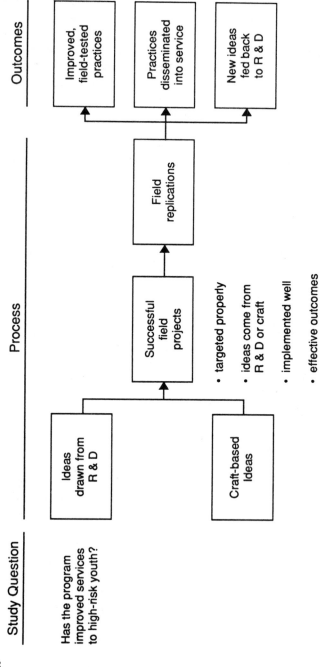

Figure 5.4. High-Risk Youth Demonstration Program: Illustrative Design

(a) African-American infants are more than twice as likely (than White or Hispanic infants) to be born with low birth weight; (b) nearly 45% of African-American children are raised in families below the poverty line (compared with 15% of White children); and (c) more African-American males (aged 18-24) are in the U.S. criminal justice system than are attending U.S. postsecondary schools of any sort. A special concern of any national effort would therefore have to be a focus on the social and economic conditions faced by African Americans in this country.

The evaluation might enumerate the various efforts undertaken to relieve these conditions or to ameliorate their effects. Such efforts would not necessarily have been part of a unified strategy or intervention but might be the agglomeration of initiatives supported by a variety of agencies and organizations, including these:

- Federal agencies, such as:
  U.S. Department of Education
  U.S. Department of Health and Human Services
  U.S. Department of Labor
  U.S. Department of Justice
- State and local agencies
- Local organizations, including:
  Community organizations
  The United Way
- National foundations, such as:
  The Annie E. Casey Foundation
  J. M. Field Foundation
  Robert Wood Johnson Foundation
  Henry J. Kaiser Family Foundation
  The Pew Charitable Trusts

In this type of case study, no evaluation could enumerate all of the existing efforts, much less classify the interventions associated with each effort. Nevertheless, the case study at this level of analysis could still be invaluable in dealing with pressing questions regarding the country's commitment to and investment in dealing with high-risk youth, the state of the art of the country's efforts, and the collective effectiveness of these efforts. The evaluation could monitor social indicators of the well-being of youth over time, anticipating a rise in such well-being as a function of a concerted national effort. Again, such an evaluation would differ dramatically from evaluations focusing on other units of analysis, as previously described.

A SUMMARY FRAMEWORK

Figure 5.5 summarizes the different units of analysis and the steps required to develop appropriate case study designs for each unit. The figure is intended first to demonstrate that each row entails a different evaluation study and that these studies will call for different designs, data collection activities, and reports. Second, each column of the figure is intended to call attention to the steps to be followed in developing a design, regardless of the row.

Six Design Steps. The columns suggest at least six steps in the design process. *First,* you should begin with the identification of the study questions. The preceding discussion of different units of analysis has provided examples of these questions and also has indicated how differences among these questions depend on and determine the unit of analysis. Moreover, this relationship between the study questions and the subsequent study is so strong that should the study questions change substantially during the conduct of a study—you might have to start the design and conduct of the evaluation study all over again. Such a feature is contrary to uninformed views of case study designs—in which research sponsors believe that study questions can be readily changed midstream, because of a case study's "flexibility." In fact, you should resist such midstream changes because they are likely to jeopardize the integrity and quality of your entire case study, unless you are given the time and resources to start all over again.

Second, your design must entertain the possibility of other units of analysis also being relevant and different from the main unit of analysis. In an evaluation of a high-risk youth project, for instance, the project could be the main unit of analysis but individual youths might be another (embedded) unit of analysis. You will follow different data collection and analysis strategies for each different unit of analysis.

Third, your design should include the procedures and rationale for selecting the specific cases to be studied. This step might occur before or after the *fourth* step—the identification of relevant outcomes and of theories and rival theories to explain these outcomes (Yin, 1984/1989). The outcomes, theories, and rival theories would constitute the substance of your evaluation design. The most desired design would have rich, mutually exclusive patterns of events predicted by a theory and its rival. You could then compare the observed pattern of empirical data to both predicted patterns, to determine the better match (see next paragraph).

Steps in Developing the Design

Unit of Analysis	Study Questions (1)	Other Possible Units of Analysis (2)	Selection of Case(s) (3)	Relevant Outcomes	Casual Logic (4)	Rival Logics	Sources of Evidence (5)	Analytic Strategies (6)
Individual								
Project								
Organization								
Program								
National Effort								

Figure 5.5. Framework for Developing Case Study Designs

91

Fifth and *sixth,* your case study design should point to the likely sources of evidence and the analytic strategies to be used. Prominent among these analytic strategies is a pattern-matching technique—discussed in greater detail in Chapter 4—which matches an observed (empirical) pattern to a predicted (theoretical) pattern. As but one classic example, this type of pattern-matching was conducted by Campbell in his example of the traffic-fatality effects of the 1955 reduction in Connecticut's state speed limit (Campbell, 1969). Alternatively, your pattern-matching might follow the "nonequivalent dependent variables" design described by Cook and Campbell (1979). Finally, your pattern-matching might try to match across (predicted and observed) independent and dependent variables simultaneously.

How the Program Dictates the Design. This discussion of high-risk youth programs shows how different case study designs must be developed, depending on the unit of analysis. In turn, the main unit of analysis depends on the study questions that have been posited. Explanatory case studies can then be designed, with precise measurement of outcomes and with inferential testing of causal theories and rival theories. These procedures do not differ from those undertaken in any scientific endeavor.

Most studies of high-risk youth programs will be interested in causal theories at the level of the individual youth—how risk factors may be reduced or how early interventions might prevent later undesired behavior, such as dropping out from school, starting drugs, or becoming economically dependent on welfare systems. If the programmatic questions and theories are of this nature, the individual youth remains the unit of analysis, even though an evaluation may focus on a specific project or even program. However, if a study is interested in project, organizational, program, or national performance—and why such performance might be deemed successful or wanting—entirely different questions, theories, and designs would be needed.

In this sense, the definition of the program of interest defines the design to be used. You need to be sensitive to these implicit choices to assure the conduct of high-quality case study evaluations.

EXERCISES

1. *Distinguishing case study, experimental, and quasi-experimental designs.* Define a topic for a case study evaluation. How many "subjects" or data points does the evaluation have? How many variables of interest, to be measured as part of the evaluation? Can the evaluator manipulate these variables? How can you be

sure that you have identified a case study evaluation and not an evaluation that can be done with either experimental or quasi-experimental methods?

2. *Defining the units of analysis for an evaluation.* Cite a different case study evaluation study for each of the following units of analysis: an evaluation of a project; an evaluation of an organization; an evaluation of a program; and an evaluation of a national effort. Again, how can you be sure that you have cited case study evaluations?

3. *Identifying rival theories.* For any one of the preceding evaluation studies you have cited, describe the program theory underlying the intervention. Now see if you can describe a rival theory that also is applicable. Are the two theories mutually exclusive?

4. *Replicating a case study evaluation.* For another one of the evaluation studies you identified in Question 2 above, describe how a subsequent evaluation could be designed to replicate the results of the first evaluation. In the subsequent evaluation, what is being replicated?

6

Lessons Learned About the Effects of Community-Based Prevention Programs

The preceding two chapters have made one fundamental assumption: that a given intervention can be adequately covered by a single evaluation design and single study. The chapters have therefore presented the various options for selecting these designs and studies, by comparing different evaluation methods (Chapter 4) and by comparing different types of programs (Chapter 5). This chapter challenges this fundamental assumption. In some situations, no single design or study may be adequate to evaluate the intervention. Yet, the strategy of deliberately using multiple studies in the same evaluation has not been part of the traditional evaluation literature. Therefore, this closing chapter attempts to point to a potentially emerging trend in evaluation research. The eventual "case study" evaluation would be the collection of this entire set of multiple studies.

The candidate substantive topic for using this strategy is substance abuse prevention. A review of progress by existing prevention efforts suggests that although substance abuse prevention efforts have become more comprehensive and community-based in order to be effective, the needed strategies for evaluating these efforts are only still being developed. Further, such strategies evaluation also might be useful for assessing all community-based programs, not just those dealing with substance abuse prevention.

AUTHOR'S NOTE: This chapter is adapted from a report originally coauthored with William J. Sabol, "Learning About the Effects of Community-Based Prevention: A Progress Report," COSMOS Corporation, 1990. A version also was presented with Katharine Zantal-Wiener at a conference, "New Directions in Child and Family Research: Shaping Head Start in the Nineties," sponsored by the U.S. Administration for Children, Youth, and Families, Washington, DC, June 26, 1991.

SUBSTANCE ABUSE PREVENTION:
TARGETING BOTH INDIVIDUAL AND ENVIRONMENT

Substance abuse prevention may be defined as actions intended to dissuade a nonuser from experimenting with alcohol and other substances abused—including the use of tobacco, marijuana, alcohol, and the variety of illicit drugs now on the market. Such actions, however, may be aimed either solely at the at-risk individual or at the individual along with the social and broader environment within which the individual lives. Successful prevention programs and community efforts are increasingly targeting both types of actions. This broader strategy is based on a public health model of prevention (Albee, 1987) and differs significantly from prevention models focusing only on the high-risk individual. When prevention is aimed at the individual only, the implicit paradigm still is a "treatment" paradigm—based on the assumption that treating an individual with some "dosage" of prevention will produce the desired outcome. In contrast, the fuller prevention models must assume that many important, ultimate outcomes must involve social groupings and the social environment, not just the individual (Holder & Giesbrecht, 1990; Wittman, 1990).

As but one example, for women much more than men, "connections" to other individuals may be a critical aspect of the social environment. Healthy connections are empowering and lead to the development of yet more connections. Women denied the opportunity to develop healthy connections may be those that are most vulnerable to substance abuse (Finkelstein, 1990). Thus the most effective substance-abuse prevention strategies may be those that include strategies aimed at reinforcing these connections and networks rather than aimed just at the individuals in need.

Another example derives from research on the "supply side" of substance abuse. In this regard, investigations of the illicit drug trade are difficult to conduct and confirm. However, less difficult is research on alcohol products (Holder, 1987). Not surprisingly, studies of the alcohol beverage industry (e.g., Morgan, 1988; Room, 1987) have readily demonstrated the multiple ways in which the industry has sought to affect the market environment and social environment, not just individual motivations. The industry has organized to promote a favorable image of alcohol (Morgan, 1988) as well as favorable marketing conditions. Similar strategies have been followed by the tobacco industry.

Figure 6.1 illustrates the broader view of prevention by noting the relevance of marketplace factors, laws, the role of the media, law enforcement and school policies, as well as community, parent, peer, and individual factors (OSAP, 1989b). Similarly, an enumeration of the pertinent "risk factors" associated with high-risk individuals reveals that only some of these factors are totally confined to the individual—that is, intrapersonal factors (Goplerud, 1989; OSAP, 1990b). Other factors involve the individual's relationships with other persons—interpersonal factors—and yet other factors deal with the environment—extrapersonal factors (Goplerud, 1989; OSAP, 1990b). As a result, successful prevention programs must show an ability to affect all of these three types of factors as ultimate outcomes, not just individual factors.

WHAT ARE WE LEARNING ABOUT PREVENTION?

Recent research, demonstration, and evaluation results point to five overall findings, given this broader prevention strategy. Much of the information comes from activities supported by the U.S. Office for Substance Abuse Prevention (OSAP), including reviews of such programs by the U.S. General Accounting Office (1990).

Impact on the At-Risk Individual. First, within schools and communities, specific educational programs have repeatedly replicated earlier research and demonstrated positive prevention outcomes with at-risk youths (Botvin, 1990). These are programs based on proactive participation—such as some combination of resistance skills training (first developed by Evans, 1976; see also Evans et al., 1978), life skills training, or social competence training (e.g., Botvin, 1986; DiCicco et al., 1984; Ellickson and Bell, 1990; Higgins, 1988; Hopkins, Mauss, Kearney, & Weisheit, 1988)—also characterized sometimes in terms of a "social influence" model (e.g., Flay, 1985; Hansen, 1990).

The overall findings are that youths exposed to social influence models of prevention do later show reduced levels of substance abuse, especially with regard to gateway drugs (cigarettes, alcohol, and marijuana). A significant number of exemplary programs, selected in 1987, reflected this prevention approach in school systems (OSAP, 1989b). Many of the programs only targeted the youths themselves. However, the distinctive effort known as Project STAR (*S*tudents *T*aught *A*wareness and *R*esistance) also has involved parent participation, community task forces, policy changes, media coverage, and neighborhood organizing (Alexander, 1989; Pentz et al., 1986). The project started on a communitywide basis in Kansas City

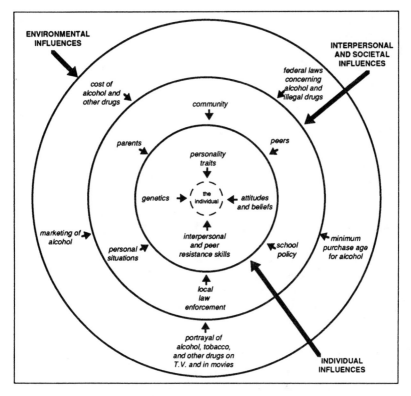

Figure 6.1. Factors That Influence Alcohol and Other Drug Use
SOURCE: OSAP, 1989b.

in 1984 and then successfully replicated itself in Indianapolis several years later.

These repeated replications do not mean that all resistance skills, life skills, or social influence efforts will demonstrate unequivocally positive results. Where the findings are neutral (but not negative), questions must still be asked about differences in implementation fidelity or the quality of the intervention (e.g., Moskowitz et al., 1983; Moskowitz et al., 1984). Other replications have shown positive intermediate outcomes but have not necessarily provided evidence on ultimate outcomes (e.g., Schuyler et al., 1985).

Impact on "Significant Others." Second, a variety of prevention efforts has demonstrated effective ways of dealing with the "significant others" of the at-risk individual. Significant others may include a person's family, peers, teachers, or counselors. To have an impact on these significant others means that a prevention program is successfully influencing the social environment—that is, the individual's social fabric. In turn, reviews have shown that programs working with this social fabric are more likely to affect positively the targeted youth and their substance-abuse behavior (Swisher, 1990). One major example of this approach is the social development model, focusing on the social bonding between family and school (Hawkins & Weiss, 1985). The model has demonstrated successful results (e.g., Hawkins et al., 1988) and is being replicated in a wide variety of places. Other cases reflecting this outcome have emerged among OSAP's high-risk grant demonstrations (OSAP, 1990a), including a Native American program, a court-mandated program, a rural program, a program for African-American single heads of households, and an urban program.

Impact on Community Structure. Yet a third outcome has been prevention programs' positive effects on community structure and community organizing. The importance of this realm has been repeatedly espoused (e.g., Kelly, 1988; Kumpfer, 1990a, 1990b; *White Paper,* 1975). Even those working with school systems also give community action the most prominent role (U.S. Department of Education, 1987).

Actual experiences in the past few years have demonstrated the positive outcomes. For instance, individual case studies of programs in Oakland, California (NIDA, 1986) and Baltimore, Maryland (Key, no date) have shown the effects on community organizing in minority-dominated communities. These two cases suggest that outcomes such as community awareness and social climate—key aspects of the environment—can be influenced by mobilization efforts that adequately recognize both political and social forces. In both of these cases, a newly formed community organization was able to develop activities involving existing agencies (e.g., schools) and volunteers in an effective manner.

Other cases also have demonstrated the successful networking of existing agencies (OSAP, 1990a). For instance, in one program aimed at youths in a rural area, in-school activities led unexpectedly to increased community awareness about the program; ultimately, schools not originally participating in the program requested to do so.

Impact on Diverse Cultural and Social Groups. Fourth, prevention programs have successfully affected different social and cultural groups, not just White, middle-class clients. Exemplary programs have now been shown in such varied settings as tribal nations; African-American communities; Hispanic communities, with bilingual components; Asian-American communities, also with bilingual components; difficult public housing projects (one of OSAP's high-risk grant demonstrations has been successful in the largest public housing project in the country); and rural, urban, and suburban areas as well as inner-city neighborhoods. In this sense, contemporary prevention programs have expanded considerably the demonstrable generalizability of various prevention initiatives.

The programs have dealt with all phases of program design, staffing and administration, and implementation in these varied communities. Individual programs are now reporting successful outcomes when these cultural aspects have been fully confronted. For example, a program aimed at Native American youths transformed the social influence approach to prevention into distinctive bicultural communications; positive results were then reported in an evaluation that used a random assignment design (Schinke et al., 1988). The OSAP high-risk grant demonstrations also have frequently reported similar outcomes (OSAP, 1990a), especially with regard to African-American groups.

All these experiences serve only to reinforce the admonishment made 15 years ago by the Domestic Council Drug Abuse Task Force—that prevention programs must address the broad developmental needs of children and youth, accounting for the major problems affecting these young people, because drug abuse does not occur in isolation (*White Paper,* 1975, p. 65). Furthermore, prevention efforts also may be influencing cultural and social groups through mass media campaigns. Although the evidence is only fragmentary (e.g., Flay & Sobel, 1983; Hewitt & Blane, 1984; Perry & Jessor, 1985), media campaigns can influence substance-abuse attitudes and behavior.

Impact on Emerging Drug Problems. Fifth, prevention programs have successfully demonstrated their ability to deal with emerging drug problems, even when the pace of social change has been rapid. Among the problems related to crack cocaine, surfacing only in the late 1980s, was the emergence of a new victim: the infant of a crack-cocaine-abusing woman (U.S. General Accounting Office, 1990). Researchers are still trying to estimate the size of this infant population, with estimates varying as a reflection of different methods (Chasnoff, Landress, & Barrett, 1990).

Although researchers are still working on definitive information about the developmental problems of drug-exposed babies (e.g., Schneider, Griffith, & Chasnoff, 1989), prevention programs already have been put into place, with some signs of early success. For example, the U.S. Department of Health and Human Services' Office of the Inspector General has already identified 20 model programs worthy of dissemination (Kusserow, 1990a, 1990b), based on its field assessments. All the programs are aimed at reducing substance abuse before and during pregnancy and thereby leading to healthy infants. The rapidity with which new prevention programs have been produced and appear to be taking effect has been another positive outcome for prevention programs.

An Overall Pattern: Comprehensive Prevention Programs. Together, these five findings also point to an important overall pattern: that prevention efforts will be more successful where the program has intensity and breadth. Colloquially, this intensity and breadth have been labeled a program's "dosage." The higher the dosage, the more positive the outcome. Although differences in prevention activities make it impossible to state any criterion or threshold level as a goal, the relationship between dosage and outcome has been demonstrated in at least two ways, the first reflecting the *intensity* of the dosage and the second reflecting its *breadth*.

Some evaluations have been able to compare the effects of different dosages within similar settings (intensity). An illustrative example comes from a statewide evaluation of school-based prevention efforts (Scheurich, 1990). The evaluators observed that the more involved a school and community were in the effort, the more positive the impact was on student and other drug use. Specific attention was given to "high-activity" and "low-activity" schools. The high-activity schools involved substantial commitment to prevention and "an almost unbelievable number of volunteer hours." The low-activity schools involved minimal commitment and episodic efforts. Although both types of schools were shown to have similar baseline conditions, the high-activity schools later demonstrated more positive outcomes than the low-activity schools.

Other findings have shown that the more a prevention program is community- rather than merely school-based, the more positive the outcomes (breadth). School-based programs also have been shown to be more effective when they involve parents and not just students. Two examples of such positive outcomes have been the evaluations of Project PATHE (Gottfredson, 1986) and Project SMART (Hansen, 1990). In other cases, more comprehensive community efforts may attempt to integrate significant role individuals and role models in the community, spread information more broadly throughout the community, and even influence local policies (Benard, 1990).

PREVENTION EVALUATION:
WHAT IS NEEDED?

Lessons about prevention evaluation also have begun to surface. For the purpose of laying the groundwork for planning future initiatives, three lessons may be considered important.

Oversimplified Nature of Process Components of Evaluations. The first is that current evaluation guidance oversimplifies the process component of evaluations. In part, this is because the process component developed belatedly, compared to the outcome component of evaluations—see Box 16. The traditional framework did not even originally account for the process of implementing the program intervention, focusing solely on individual (or client) outcomes (see Figure 6.2).

BOX 16
Process Evaluations

An intervention or program is considered a *process,* which ideally then yields the desired outcomes. The process calls for a complex set of activities, and thus may itself be worthy of evaluation. In this respect, the concept of "process evaluations" (assessments of the interventions alone, and not of any outcomes) arose.

Processes occur over a discrete period of time. Case studies also traditionally trace events over time. Therefore, the case study method was initially conceived as a methodology for doing process evaluations (assessing whether the intervention had been implemented as planned) but not necessarily as useful for doing outcome evaluations. Traditionally, the conduct of a rigorous outcome evaluation was considered as needing unassailable quantitative data—not normally accepted as being part of a case study.

The concepts espoused in this book are different. Case study evaluations can cover both process and outcomes and can include both quantitative and qualitative data. But whether you use case studies or not, you should not settle for doing a process evaluation only. Rarely is anyone interested in the fidelity or implementation of a process alone. We all are or should be concerned with outcomes, too.

Contemporary prevention evaluation handbooks (e.g., Hawkins & Nederhood, 1987) still do not attend much to process topics. Yet, the preceding summary of prevention findings has shown how prevention

A Single Prevention Program Can Contain:

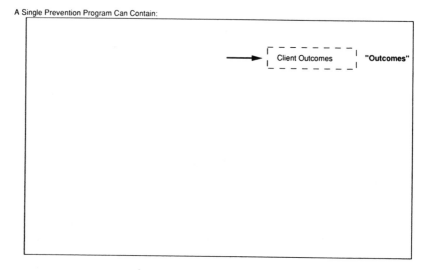

Figure 6.2. Traditional Evaluation Framework

programs are successfully incorporating complex community interventions and involve multiple program components. Simply put, the process components of evaluation models have lagged behind in addressing the complications produced by advances in prevention programs (Schaps et al., 1982). Such advances have been recognized in related fields, such as community crime prevention (Yin, 1986), but not yet in substance-abuse prevention.

In practice, the quality of process evaluations has varied. In some prevention evaluations, even though the process component was central to the evaluation, the final evaluation report either relegated it to a minor role or did not try to explain program outcomes in relation to specific program components (e.g., Ellickson & Bell, 1990). In other cases, process evaluation has been used more purposively. For instance, the evaluation of the COMPRI project—a series of six demonstrations in Alameda County, California—heavily depends on a process component designed to assist in the diffusion of knowledge and the development and evolution of the programs (Cherry & Wittman, 1990). Yet other evaluations have integrated outcome information into the intervention process. This was done in Evans's (1976) study of resistance-skills training in preventing smoking among high school youths. The study design incorporated information on the self-report rates of cigarette consumption into the intervention and subsequent process evaluation: The information was reported to

---

BOX 17
A Case Study Covering Multiple Substudies

You have seen how a case study ought to be about a single unit of analysis—an organization, a program, a project, a group, an individual, and so on. This chapter raises the possibility that your single-case study may nevertheless consist of multiple substudies. Each substudy might have its own design and data, but the logic connecting these substudies would refer back to the larger unit of analysis, or case.

Multiple substudies make sense when a single topic is so diverse that multiple processes and outcomes are at work. Different substudies are needed to focus on these diverse pairs of processes and outcomes, but the substudies as a whole are still part of the same case study. Further, some substudies may collect highly quantitative data, whereas other substudies may collect highly qualitative data. The strength of the ultimate, single-case study is whether these substudies follow some logical arrangement. For instance, if each substudy deals with a different threat to internal validity, the collection of substudies—the whole case study—may have aggregate evidence of a compelling sort. This is one way of thinking about the case studies that you might be doing in the future.

---

students at regular intervals in order to change perceptions about the schoolwide norms regarding smoking.

One of the best examples of an appropriately complex process evaluation is the ongoing evaluation of the Pawtucket Heart Health Program, an 11-year project started in 1980. As part of the evaluation, the evaluators have installed a process evaluation "system" (McGraw et al., 1989), not just a process evaluation component. The system consists of multiple data collection efforts and recognizes the complexity of a communitywide intervention by having multiple data collection efforts.

Need for Single Evaluations With Multiple Substudies. A second lesson is that to evaluate a single but complex prevention program adequately, the use of multiple substudies may be needed (see Box 17).

The possible need for multiple substudies within a singular evaluation effort has been strongly raised by the development of community-based prevention programs. For instance, Loers and Sarata (1983) captured this issue well in their description of the Pioneer Mental Health Center intervention and evaluation in Nebraska. They distinguished between "program" oriented and "community" oriented prevention efforts. A program-oriented effort can have individual or group outcomes as ultimate objectives. The objectives to be assessed will likely focus on individual measures of behavior, attitude, and participation in the program. In contrast, a community-oriented effort has as its main objective the changing of the very framework of community or social rules. System change is therefore the ultimate objective, and assessment should focus on such items as instances of community organization and activities, membership and goal of community efforts, the capability of groups for continued development, and legal and policy changes. Both program-oriented and community-oriented substudies would be needed to assess the overall impact of a prevention effort.

Another rationale for multiple substudies is when a prevention program involves multiple units of analysis. Such multiple units of analysis have been formally recognized in prevention programs (Cook, 1985)—for example, the individual, the family, the classroom, the school, and the entire school system. This view differs from the standard view of prevention involving only individuals as the unit of analysis (e.g., Moskowitz, 1989). Because different units of analysis may all be relevant in the same prevention program, and because different units are unlikely to be accommodated by the same evaluation design, multiple substudies may be needed for more complicated prevention programs.

A community-oriented prevention program would clearly represent one example of this more complicated prevention program. Yet another example would be statewide prevention programs, whose evaluation needs have received little attention. For instance, one study of an Iowa substance-abuse prevention program simply found no previous evaluations of statewide systems (Anderson, Maypole, & Norris-Henderson, 1987). The absence of such evaluations or any guidance about how to do them is intolerable, in the face of the possibility that statewide programs could be a relevant and potent approach to prevention.

Figure 6.3 illustrates how a single evaluation might be conceived as including multiple substudies. Each of the five rows might be a separate study, with its own research design, unit of analysis, and data collection activity. A significant realization is that these five assessments also accommodate the conceptualization of a prevention program as having multiple outcomes of interest (Best et al., 1989). For instance, the assessment of social interactions (e.g., "connections") and group norms may be outcomes as important as measurable changes in individual attitudes and behavior.

In this configuration of multiple substudies, the overall evaluation might be considered a single case study. Each substudy could therefore be based

A Single Education Program Can Contain:

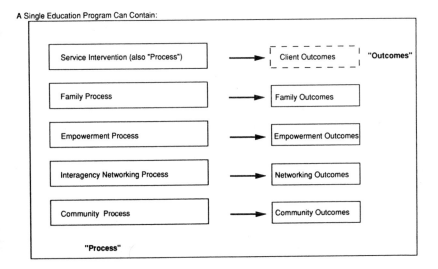

Figure 6.3. A Single Evaluation: Multiple Studies and Multiple Designs

on different units of analysis with independent data collection and analysis strategies if needed. However, the overall evaluation (case study) design would require a comprehensive rationale based on theory and policy—so that the selection of substudies made sense and their lessons could aggregate to overall findings about the single community prevention program. The designs for selecting these substudies have yet to be worked out. As an initial principle, each substudy might cover a different "threat" to internal validity.

From a prevention perspective, a comparison between Figures 6.2 and 6.3 suggests a deeper transition, beyond simply expanding from a single- to a multiple-substudy framework. Most prevention evaluations based on the traditional, client-oriented study (Figure 6.2) are in fact also built around a "treatment" design involving individual participants. Basically, the prevention intervention is considered a way of treating the high-risk individuals in the prevention activity. However, the shift to multiple substudies with multiple outcomes (Figure 6.3) may in fact also be a shift to a genuine "prevention" design, with the recognition that the complexity of community-based prevention programs inevitably requires multiple substudies with multiple outcomes (Best et al., 1989).

Figure 6.4 summarizes this possible transition by tracing the evolution of evaluation study designs from (a) a target on client outcomes alone, to

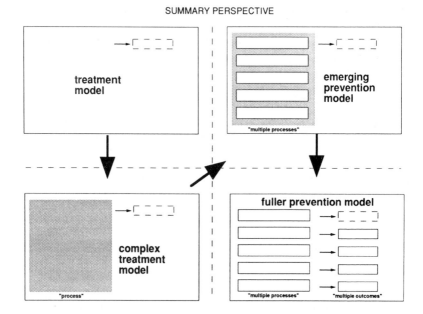

Figure 6.4. The Evolution of Evaluation Study Designs

(b) a generalized appreciation for process conditions, to (c) a refined appreciation for process components, and finally to (d) a recognition that different process components may have their own outcomes and therefore require multiple substudies.

Need to Develop Better Collaboration in Managing Evaluations. A third lesson is the need to improve the ways in which evaluators collaborate with an intervention's project managers. The key objective is to make evaluations serve as a management tool for learning about interventions, and not to permit the evaluations to become independent pieces of research (Nowakowski, 1986; Springer, 1990).

The potential problems are raised by the general noncongruence of interests between evaluators—who come from an academic community with incentives to achieve publishable results—and intervention project managers—who come from a practice community with incentives to serve clients and make a program work. When a community-based program is involved, yet a third party—the community member—also becomes involved, and the relationships among all three parties can be unstable and mismatched (Room, 1990). In prevention, a further complication is the need to integrate cultural sensitivities (Orlandi, 1986). Both the evaluator and the intervention project manager must show such sensitivities. As pointed out in one review (Futterman, 1990):

> The development of cultural competence is an essential component in the successful evaluation of substance abuse prevention programs for ethnic populations. Successful evaluations will be those which meet standard methodological criteria . . . , and which take into account the specific circumstances and context of the ethnic populations.

The potential insight here is that "cultural competence" may be a critical skill—equal in importance to the methodological and quantitative skills often considered necessary for evaluators (Futterman, 1990) or to the managerial and substantive skills considered necessary for the intervention's project managers.

Overall, evaluators and intervention managers therefore have a considerable challenge. Their collaboration is just now being given increasing attention in the prevention field and its guidebooks (e.g., Giesbrecht et al., 1990). However, some evaluation handbooks largely overlook this issue (e.g., Hawkins & Nederhood, 1987), and awareness of the problem and guidance for appropriate behaviors is only now emerging. One early handbook (French, Fisher, & Costa, 1983) focused heavily on the relationship, as reflected by its title: *Working With Evaluators: A Guide for Drug Abuse Prevention Program Managers*. Similarly, relevant methodological and managerial lessons are captured in another OSAP document, entitled "Collaborative Evaluation" (OSAP, 1989a).

Despite these promising beginnings, more needs to be done about articulating the collaborative process. The process should not only focus on individuals but also include collaboration between evaluation-based institutions and demonstration-based institutions.

SUMMARY

Substance abuse prevention efforts have demonstrated successful results, in a variety of ways. The successful strategies call for a comprehensive approach, in which prevention efforts try to deal with both the at-risk individual and the individual's social and physical environment. The evaluation of prevention programs has lagged these favorable developments. The traditional evaluation design has been oriented to the at-risk individual. However, the emerging need is to assess multiple prevention components with multiple outcomes. A singular, case study evaluation—incorporating multiple substudies—may be a viable strategy to deal with this situation. The development of such an evaluation strategy—as well as attention to effective collaboration between researcher and manager—would be a significant step toward a genuine prevention evaluation paradigm.

For case study evaluations, this same development may be applicable to a broad array of topics. A continuing challenge is to recognize when multiple substudies may be appropriate and to work out the logic to connect these substudies. A compelling logic, along with well-conducted substudies, would then indeed lead to a compelling case study.

EXERCISES

1. *Evaluations of prevention activities.* If you were doing a study of some aspect of prevention—for instance, crime prevention, drug abuse prevention, or school dropout prevention—what would be the scope of your evaluation? How far afield would you go to recognize environmental and societal conditions?

2. *Cultural sensitivity.* Cite an example where a social science method would vary, depending on the cultural or ethnic group being studied. Do you think that instruments and methods should be culturally specific, or should they be universal and ignore cultural and ethnic differences? Why?

3. *Intervention dosage.* Define intervention *dosage.* Do you think that most interventions have sufficient dosage to produce the desired results? Whether yes or no, what can be done to increase the dosage of most interventions (name specific tactics)?

4. *Process evaluation.* Define the *process* component of an evaluation. Why is this component important? How is a process evaluation best designed, and what data are typically the most relevant?

5. *Multiple substudies.* Can you cite a study—in the experimental and nonexperimental literature—that consisted of multiple substudies? If so, do you feel that this is a particularly strong study, compared to one with no such substudies? Why?

Summing Up

The preceding chapters have presented a broad array of applications of case study research. You will not likely read this type of "applications" book from cover to cover. Hopefully, you will have found a topic or chapter of immediate interest, and you will return to other topics or chapters at some later time. Nevertheless, what are the really important points that this book raises? This "summing up" tries to cover a few.

POSING STUDY QUESTIONS AND ISSUES
BEFORE PROCEEDING FURTHER

Of all the lessons learned about doing case studies, the most important is to develop the initial study questions and issues—as fully as possible—before doing anything else. Narrowly, these questions should focus on substantive concerns. Broadly, they also can include the practical resources and limitations involved in your study—and your study plan. Figure B.1 presents this more comprehensive picture, shared with me by a Danish colleague, Professor Finn Borum (1991) of the University of Copenhagen. The figure shows the complete process to be planned in doing a case study —from initial design to data collection, analysis, and report. However, let's focus mainly on the narrow, substantive concerns for the moment (what the figure shows as the Research Objectives and Questions oval).

The preceding chapters have given many examples of the importance of defining the topics of study carefully—including identifying relevant literatures, hypotheses, and units of analysis. Chapter 1 deals in its entirety with the importance of defining the initial study questions. The chapter emphasizes the role of "theorizing" about a case study before proceeding further. Examples are given of how to theorize about exploratory, descriptive, and causal case studies, and even of how to specify substantive issues to guide the case selection process. Similarly, Chapters 2 and 3 on education and management information systems give ample attention to the problem of defining the initial units of analysis prior to conducting a case study. As final examples, Chapter 5 shows how entirely different evaluations

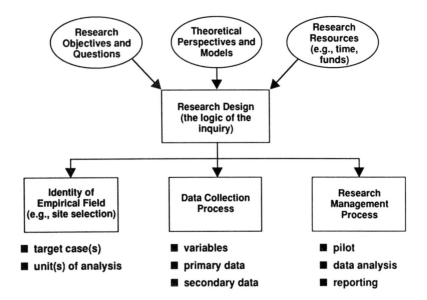

Figure B.1. The Central Function of a Research Design
Source: Borum, 1991

will be conducted, depending on the definition of the program to be evaluated, and Chapter 6 shows how technical findings in substance-abuse prevention—drawn from the literature in that field—will influence the broad design of any ensuing evaluation.

All these examples are intended to show how to target your case study before you actually start conducting it. The targeting process is no different from that used in all scientific studies—where a review of the literature begets key hypotheses to be tested, which in turn become the focus of data collection and analysis. In case studies, the targeting is essential. First, you will know that you have a target, and you are therefore more likely to complete your case study. Second, you will hope that your defined target is critical to the substantive field of interest, and that your case study will therefore contribute to the cumulative body of knowledge in that field.

Where investigators most encounter trouble in doing case studies is where the study questions and issues have not been well defined. My recommendation is that investigators spend intensive—even compulsive— effort at this stage. Recommended activities include thorough reviews of the literature as well as dialogues (indeed, debates) with colleagues and research sponsors to clarify the issues. If you cannot defend the rationale for your study to a colleague, you also are not likely to do a good case study.

JUMPING DIRECTLY INTO DATA COLLECTION

The admonition to define study questions and issues early does have an exception, however. Sometimes, an important case presents itself and the appropriate case study design seems almost predefined. In other situations, data collection might have to start before the investigator has had a chance to define the study questions and issues properly. The preceding chapters have presented examples of these situations, too. Chapter 1 includes a descriptive study of categorical and noncategorical education, where states were practicing certain policies in need of study. Chapter 3 mentions a hypothetical MIS software that in fact could already have existed and would become the subject of a case study. Similarly, some important demonstration project could have been in need of a case study evaluation in Chapter 4. Finally, Chapter 4 also suggests how a youth gang problem might emerge rather quickly, requiring early study (the National Science Foundation actually has a formalized program for doing rapid case studies of natural disasters—in which investigators are sent into the field within hours, if possible, of the occurrence of the disaster).

So, we can all cite instances where the intensive and lengthy devotion to clarifying study questions and issues ahead of time may not occur. Figure B.2 diagrams this situation by deviating from the original conceptualization by my colleague Finn Borum, indicating a nonlinear path. In this path, the selection of the case(s)—for whatever reason—precedes the development of the study questions and issues. In spite of the earlier insistence on posing study issues before proceeding further, this nonlinear path may in fact be followed—under certain circumstances—in doing a case study.

The main acceptable circumstances are where the case study is to be conducted by an experienced investigator. Thus a major warning is that only an experienced investigator is likely to be successful in following the nonlinear path. If you are *in*experienced—either in doing empirical research in general or in carrying out studies in your substantive topic—the chances are high that the nonlinear path will lead to a poorly conceived case study and an unhappy outcome. The experienced investigator will use his or her prior knowledge to make early choices in design or data collection that will later pay off, even though a formal review of the literature—or issues development phase—has not been undertaken. The experienced investigator will know how to leave certain avenues of inquiry open and how to collect the relevant data if they must be collected early, without leaving the study vulnerable to later accusations of bias.

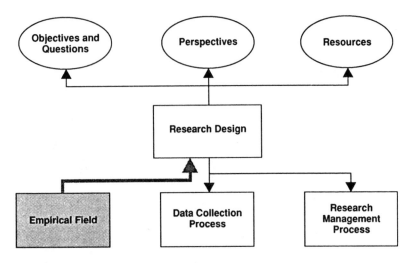

Figure B.2. Field Access Opportunism

An example would be an evaluation in which a demonstration project starts on its own schedule, not awaiting the preparation time needed by the case study investigator. Some investigators, following my first recommendation, would nevertheless take the preparation time to define the study questions and issues, and therefore start data collection after the demonstration had already been under way for some time. A more experienced investigator would know that some baseline measurements would later be invaluable and, even though the specific study design had not yet been completed, would initiate data collection with the start of the demonstration project. The experiential factor would allow the investigator to follow some hunches about what data might be important later. The experiential factor would also mean that the evaluation would roughly target the key policy issues, even if started quickly.

USING RIVALS AS A MEANS OF QUALITY CONTROL

Another important summary point is the benefit of using rival hypotheses and rival theories—indeed, rival or contrary thinking—as a means of adding quality control to your case study. Many times, I have been asked how to assure that a case study can avoid bias, whether in its initial formulation, its data collection, its data analysis, or even in its reporting.

In every instance, my answer has been to encourage rival thinking that is serious, open, and fair.

The preceding chapters have identified several rival situations, also showing how they can be derived from different sources. Chapter 1 describes an illustrative study of high-tech versus industrial parks. These rival considerations derived from actual practices and policies in place in locales around the country. Chapter 1 also cites another study on research utilization, showing how the previous research literature had promoted three major rival theories, and how these became the guidelines for the subsequent case study. Chapter 3 presents a simple set of rival hypotheses about the successful implementation of MIS systems based primarily on the experiences of previous management consultants who had observed the rivals in practice—managers typically start by only considering the MIS as a technology to be implemented, and only later understand that the entire organization might have to be reorganized. Finally, Chapter 5 contains a brief allusion to rival theories of the role and importance of demonstration programs in helping to translate existing findings from laboratory research into practical applications in the field.

These are all instances of formal, rival hypotheses or theories. They are all plausible rivals. The effect of articulating them at the outset of a case study is to influence the design and data collection of the study. Ideally, the case study will fairly collect the data needed to give each rival an opportunity to be proven correct or incorrect. If these procedures are carried out properly, the study will not only contribute to the substantive literature but also have incorporated key procedures to avoid pitfalls regarding biased results.

More such thinking needs to be incorporated at every step in designing and doing your case studies. Some rivals may be derived from simple argument. A colleague of yours may be critical of your proposed case study design because it does not rule out a particular interpretation. (Recently, someone asked me how I could be sure that the results from four case studies would not be limited to the ethnic groups being studied, and how I could be sure that the findings would apply to Latino groups—that might not be among the groups in the four cases.) You should treat the criticism as a potential rival. Then, ask your colleague (and yourself) what data could be collected in order to assess this interpretation. At this pre-data collection stage, you and your colleague should assume perfect data collection and logically determine whether the design will be able to test the interpretation. The interesting result is not only to reduce subsequent bias but also to translate every challenge into an operational plan for data collection, interpretation, and analysis.

EXTENDING THE APPLICABILITY
OF THE CASE STUDY METHOD

A final summary point is to note how all the applications presented in this book focus on some organizational but not individual or small group issue. The applications in Chapters 1-6 cover such phenomena as organizational performance, policy interventions, project implementation, organizations' relationships with other organizations, and program development. Yet, one of the original motives for using case studies was to study individuals or small groups of people in depth (see, e.g., Chapter 5). Because my own research has been largely limited to organizational phenomena, other investigators will have to determine whether many of the principles espoused under organizational conditions also apply to the study of individuals and small groups. In this sense, we are still in need of continually testing the generalizability (external validity) of the case study methods presented in this book. In a way, every successful case study—including your own—represents a similar test of the method. Hopefully, your test will be successful.

References

Albee, George W. (1987). Powerlessness, politics, and prevention: The community mental health approach. In Klaus Hurrelman et al. (Eds.), *Social intervention: Potential and constraints* (pp. 37-52). New York: Walter de Gruyter.

Alexander, Patricia. (1989, September). Comprehensive community drug abuse prevention program. In *Hearings,* Committee on Labor and Human Resources, U.S. Senate, 101st Congress, 1st Session, pp. 25-41.

Alkin, Marvin C., et al. (1979). *Using evaluations: Does evaluation make a difference?* Beverly Hills, CA: Sage.

Allison, Graham T. (1971) *Essence of decision: Explaining the Cuban missile crisis.* Boston: Little, Brown.

Anderson, Ruth B., Maypole, Donald E., & Norris-Henderson, Karen. (1987). A model for the evaluation of statewide substance abuse prevention programs. *The International Journal of the Addictions, 22*(10), 917-925.

Baer, Walter S., Johnson, Leland S., & Merrow, Edward W. (1976, April). *Analysis of federally funded demonstration projects.* Santa Monica, CA: The Rand Corporation.

Belk, Russell W., Sherry, John F., Jr., & Wallendorf, Melanie. (1988, March). A naturalistic inquiry into buyer and seller behavior at a swap meet. *Journal of Consumer Research, 14,* 449-470.

Benard, Bonnie. (1990). An overview of community-based prevention. In Ketty H. Rey et al. (Eds.), *Prevention research findings, 1988* (pp. 126-147). Rockville, MD: Office for Substance Abuse Prevention.

Benbasat, I., Goldstein, D., & Mead, M. (1987, September). The case research strategy in studies of information systems. *MIS Quarterly, 11,* 369-386.

Berk, Richard A., & Rossi, Peter H. (1990). *Thinking about program evaluation.* Newbury Park, CA: Sage.

Berman, Paul, & McLaughlin, Milbrey. (1976, March). Implementation of educational innovation. *The Educational Forum, 40,* 347-370.

Best, J. Allan, et al. (1989). Conceptualizing outcomes for health promotion programs. In Marc T. Braverman (Ed.), *Evaluating health promotion programs* (pp. 33-45). San Francisco: Jossey-Bass.

Bickman, Leonard. (1987). The functions of program theory. In L. Bickman (Ed.), *Using program theory in evaluation: New directions for program evaluation* (pp. 5-18). San Francisco: Jossey-Bass.

Borum, Finn. (1991). Personal communication. Copenhagen, Denmark: Copenhagen Business School.

Botvin, Gilbert J. (1986, November). Substance abuse prevention research: Recent developments and future directions. *Journal of School Health, 56,* 369-374.

Botvin, Gilbert J. (1990). Substance abuse prevention: Theory, practice, and effectiveness. In Michael Tonry & James Q. Wilson (Eds.), *Drugs and crime* (pp. 461-519). Chicago: University of Chicago Press.

Brookover, Wilbur B. (1981). *Effective secondary schools.* Philadelphia, PA: Research for Better Schools.

Campbell, Donald T. (1969, April). Reforms as experiments. *American Psychologist, 24,* 409-429.

Campbell, Donald T. (1975, July). Degrees of freedom and the case study. *Comparative Political Studies, 8,* 178-193.

Campbell, Donald T., & Stanley, J. C. (1963). *Experimental and quasi-experimental designs for research.* Chicago: Rand McNally.

Chasnoff, Ira J., Landress, Harvey J., & Barrett, Mark E. (1990, April). The prevalence of illicit-drug or alcohol use during pregnancy and discrepancies in mandatory reporting in Pinellas County, Florida. *The New England Journal of Medicine, 322,* 1202-1206.

Chen, Huey-Tsyh. (1990). *Theory-driven evaluations.* Newbury Park, CA: Sage.

Chen, Huey-Tsyh, & Rossi, Peter H. (1989). Issues in the theory-driven perspective. *Evaluation and Program Planning, 12*(4), 299-306.

Cherry, Linda, & Wittman, Friedner D. (January 1990). *Designing and community planning and information system for alcohol program reduction: The COMPRI project.* Paper presented at the international conference Evaluating Community Prevention Strategies: Alcohol and Other Drugs, San Diego, CA.

Cohen, Michael. (1982, January/February). Effective schools: Accumulating research findings. *American Education, 18,* 13-16.

Cook, Thomas D. (1985). Priorities in research in smoking prevention. In Catherine S. Bell & Robert Battjes (Eds.), *Prevention research: Deterring drug use among children and adolescents* (pp. 196-220). Rockville, MD: National Institute on Drug Abuse.

Cook, Thomas D., & Campbell, Donald T. (1979). *Quasi-experimentation: Design and analysis issues for field settings.* Chicago: Rand McNally.

DiCicco, L., Biron, R., Carifo, J., Deutsch, C., Mills, D. J., Orenstein, A., Re, A., Unterberger, H., & White, R. E. (1984). Evaluation of the CASPAR alcohol education curriculum. *Journal of Studies on Alcohol, 45,* 160-169.

Dorr-Bremme, Donald W. (1985). Ethnographic evaluation: A theory and method. *Educational Evaluation and Policy Analysis, 7,* 65-83.

Downs, George W., Jr., & Mohr, Lawrence. (1976, December). Conceptual issues in the study of innovation. *Administrative Science Quarterly, 21,* 700-714.

Ellickson, Phyllis L., & Bell, Robert M. (1990, March). *Prospects for preventing drug use among young adolescents.* Santa Monica, CA: The Rand Corporation.

Evans, R. I. (1976). Smoking in children: Developing a social psychological strategy of deterrence. *Preventive Medicine, 5,* 122-127.

Evans, R. I., Rozelle, R. M., Mittlemark, M. B., Hansen, W. B., Bane, A. L., & Havis, J. (1978). Deterring the onset of smoking in children: Knowledge of immediate physiological effects and coping with peer pressure, media pressure, and parent modeling. *Journal of Applied Social Psychology, 8,* 126-135.

Fetterman, David. (1989). *Ethnography: Step by step.* Newbury Park, CA: Sage.

Finkelstein, Norma. (September 1990). *Treatment issues: Women and substance abuse.* Paper presented at the Conference on Healthy Women, Healthy Pregnancies, Healthy Babies, Miami, FL.

Fisher, R. A. (1935). *The Design of Experiments.* London: Oliver & Boyd.

Flay, Brian R. (1985). What we know about the social influences approach to smoking prevention: Review and recommendations. In Catherine S. Bell & Robert Battjes (Eds.), *Prevention research: Deterring drug abuse among children and adolescents* (pp. 67-112). Rockville, MD: National Institute on Drug Abuse.

Flay, Brian R., & Sobel, J. L. (1983). The role of mass media in preventing adolescent substance abuse. In T. J. Glynn et al. (Eds.), *Preventing adolescent drug abuse: Intervention strategies,* National Institute on Drug Abuse Monograph, Number 47. Washington, DC: U.S. Department of Health, Education, and Welfare.

French, John F., Fisher, Court C., & Costa, Samuel J., Jr. (Eds.). (1983). *Working with evaluators: A guide for drug abuse prevention program managers.* Rockville, MD: National Institute on Drug Abuse.

Futterman, Robert. (1990). *Cultural competence: Evaluating substance abuse prevention programs for ethnic populations.* Bibliography with annotations prepared for the Office for Substance Abuse Prevention, Rockville, MD.

George, A., & McKeown, T. (1985). Case studies and theories of organizational decision making. In L. Sproull & P. Larkey (Eds.), *Advances in information processing in organizations, Vol. 2* (pp. 21-58). Greenwich, CT: JAI Press.

Giesbrecht, Norman, et al. (Eds.). (1990). *Research, action, and the community: Experiences in the prevention of alcohol and other drug problems* (pp. 225-238). Rockville, MD: Office for Substance Abuse Prevention.

Ginsburg, Alan L. (1989, December). Revitalizing program evaluation: The U.S. Department of Education experience. *Evaluation Review, 13,* 579-597.

Glaser, Barney G., & Strauss, Anselm L. (1967). *The discovery of grounded theory: Strategies for qualitative research.* Chicago: Aldine.

Glennan, Thomas K., et al. (1978, May). *The role of demonstrations in federal r&d policy.* Santa Monica, CA: The Rand Corporation.

Goetz, Judith Preissle, & LeCompte, Margaret Diane. (1984). *Ethnography and qualitative design in educational research.* San Diego, CA: Academic Press.

Goodman, Leo A. (1978). *Analyzing qualitative/categorical data: Log-linear models and latent structure analysis.* Cambridge, MA: Abt Books.

Goodstadt, Michael. (1990). Addressing the problems of action research in the community: Lessons from alcohol and drug education. In Norman Giesbrecht et al. (Eds.), *Research, action, and the community: Experiences in the prevention of alcohol and other drug problems* (pp. 225-238). Rockville, MD: Office for Substance Abuse Prevention.

Goplerud, Eric. (1989, May). Presentation at Demand Reduction Task Force meeting, Prevention/Education Programs of ADAMHA.

Gottfredson, Don C. (1986). An empirical test of school-based environmental and individual interventions to reduce the risk of delinquent behavior. *Criminology, 24*(4), 705-730.

Gross, Neal, et al. (1971). *Implementing organizational innovations.* New York: Basic Books.

Guba, Egon G., & Lincoln, Yvonna S. (1982, Winter). Epistemological and methodological bases of naturalistic inquiry. *Educational Communications and Technology Journal, 30,* 233-252.

Gummesson, Evert. (1988). *Qualitative methods in management research.* Bickley, Bromley (UK): Chartwell-Bratt.

Hansen, William B. (1990). Theory and implementation of the social influence model of primary prevention. In Ketty H. Rey et al. (Eds.), *Prevention research findings, 1988* (pp. 93-107). Rockville, MD: Office for Substance Abuse Prevention.

Hawkins, J. David, & Nederhood, Britt. (1987). *Handbook for evaluating drug and alcohol prevention.* Rockville, MD: Office for Substance Abuse Prevention.

Hawkins, J. David, & Weiss, Joseph G. (1985). The social development model: An integrated approach to delinquency prevention. *Journal of Primary Prevention, 6,* 73-97.

Hawkins, J. David, et al. (1988). Affective and social influences approaches to the prevention of multiple substance abuse among seventh grade students: Results from Project SMART. *Preventive Medicine, 17,* 1-20.

Hedrick, Terry, Bickman, Leonard, & Rog, Debra J. (1993). *Applied research design.* Newbury Park, CA: Sage.

Hewitt, L. E., & Blane, H. T. (1984). Prevention through mass media communication. In P. M. Miller & T. D. Nirenberg (Eds.), *Prevention of alcohol abuse.* New York: Plenum Press.

Higgins, Paul S. (1988, May). *The prevention of drug abuse among teenagers: A literature review.* Unpublished paper, Amherst H. Wilder Foundation, St. Paul, MN.

Hodgkinson, Harold L. (1989). *The same client: The demographics of education and service delivery systems.* Washington, DC: Institute for Educational Leadership.

Holder, Harold D. (Ed.). (1987). *Control issues in alcohol abuse prevention: Strategies for states and communities.* Greenwich, CT: JAI Press.

Holder, Harold D., & Giesbrecht, Norman. (1990). Perspectives on the community in action research. In Norman Giesbrecht et al. (Eds.), *Research, action, and the community: Experiences in the prevention of alcohol and other drug problems* (pp. 27-44). Rockville, MD: Office for Substance Abuse Prevention.

Hopkins, R. H., Mauss, A. L., Kearney, K. A., & Weisheit, R. A. (1988). Comprehensive evaluation of a model alcohol education curriculum. *Journal of Studies on Alcohol, 49,* 38-50.

House, Ernest. (1982). Alternative evaluation strategies in higher education. In Richard F. Wilson (Ed.), *Designing academic program reviews* (pp. 5-15). San Francisco: Jossey-Bass.

Howard, Jan. (1990). Prevention research at NIAAA: Confronting the challenge of uncertainty. In Ketty H. Rey et al. (Eds.), *Prevention research findings, 1988* (pp. 243-252). Rockville, MD: Office for Substance Abuse Prevention.

Johnson, Allen W. (1978). *Quantification in cultural anthropology: An introduction to research design.* Stanford, CA: Stanford University Press.

Jorgensen, Danny. (1989). *Participant observation: A methodology for human studies.* Newbury Park, CA: Sage

Kelly, James G. (1988). *A guide to conducting prevention research in the community: First steps.* New York: The Haworth Press.

Key, Addie J. (n.d.). *Preventing alcohol/drug problems in inner-city communities: A model.* Division of Prevention Implementation, Office for Substance Abuse Prevention.

Kidder, Louise H., Judd, Charles M., & Smith, Eliot R. (1986). *Research methods in social relations,* 5th ed. New York: Holt, Rinehart & Winston.

Kids count data book: State profiles of child well-being. (1991). Washington, DC: The Center for the Study of Social Policy.

Kling, Rob, & Iacono, S. (1984, December). The control of information systems developments after implementation. *Communications of the ACM, 27,* 1218-1226.

Kumpfer, Karol L. (1990a). Challenges to prevention programs in schools: The thousand flowers must bloom. In *Prevention research findings, 1988* (pp. 108-123). Rockville, MD: Office for Substance Abuse Prevention.

Kumpfer, Karol L. (1990b). Environmental and family-focused prevention. In *Prevention research findings, 1988* (pp. 194-220). Rockville, MD: Office for Substance Abuse Prevention.

Kusserow, Richard P. (1990a, June). *Crack babies.* Washington, DC: Office of Inspector General, U.S. Department of Health and Human Services.

Kusserow, Richard P. (1990b). *Crack babies: Selected model practices.* Washington, DC: Office of Inspector General, U.S. Department of Health and Human Services.

Lee, Allen S. (1988, August). *A scientific methodology for MIS case studies.* Paper presented at annual meeting of Academy of Management, Anaheim, CA.

Leonard-Barton, Dorothy. (1987, May/June). Implementing structured software methodologies: A case of innovation in process technology. *Interfaces, 17,* 6-17.

Lightfoot, Sara Lawrence. (1983). *The good high school.* New York: Basic Books.

Lincoln, Yvonna S., & Guba, Egon G. (1985). *Naturalistic inquiry.* Newbury Park, CA: Sage.

Lincoln, Yvonna S., & Guba, Egon G. (1986). But is it rigorous? Trustworthiness and authenticity in naturalistic evaluation. In D. D. Williams (Ed.), *Naturalistic evaluation.* San Francisco: Jossey-Bass.

Loers, Deborah, & Sarata, Brian. (1983, August). *A community development model for prevention of chemical abuse.* Paper presented at the annual meeting of the American Psychological Association, Anaheim, CA.

Madaus, George F., Stufflebeam, Daniel, & Scriven, Michael S. (1989). Program evaluation: A historical overview. In Madaus, Scriven, & Stufflebeam (Eds.), *Evaluation models: Viewpoints in educational and human services evaluation* (pp. 3-22). Norwell, MA: Kluwer-Nijhoff.

Markus, M. Lynne. (1983, June). Power, politics, and MIS implementation. *Communications of the ACM, 26,* 430-444.

Maruyama, G., & Deno, S. (1992). *Research in educational settings.* Newbury Park, CA: Sage.

McCall, W. A. (1923). *How to experiment in education.* New York: Macmillan.

McGraw, Sarah A., et al. (1989, October). Methods in program evaluation: The process evaluation system of the Pawtucket Heart Health Program. *Evaluation Review, 13,* 459-483.

McLaughlin, Milbrey. (1975). *Evaluation and reform: The elementary and secondary Education Act of 1965/Title I.* Cambridge, MA: Ballinger Books.

McLaughlin, Milbrey. (1976, February). Implementation as mutual adaptation. *Teachers College Record, 77*(3).

Merriam, Sharan B. (1988). *Case study research in education: A qualitative approach.* San Francisco: Jossey-Bass.

Mohr, Lawrence. (1978, July). Process theory and variance theory in innovation research. In Michael Radnor et al. (Eds.), *The diffusion of innovations: An assessment.* Evanston, IL: Northwestern University.

Morgan, Patricia A. (1988, Summer). Power, politics and public health: The political power of the alcohol beverage industry. *Journal of Public Health Policy, 10,* 177-197.

Moskowitz, Joel M. (1989). Preliminary guidelines for reporting outcome evaluation studies of health promotion and disease prevention programs. In Marc T. Braverman (Ed.), *Evaluating health promotion programs* (pp. 101-112). San Francisco: Jossey-Bass.

Moskowitz, Joel M., et al. (1983). Evaluation of a junior high school primary prevention program. *Addictive Behaviors, 8,* 393-401.

Moskowitz, Joel M., et al. (1984). Evaluation of a substance abuse prevention program for junior high school students. *International Journal of the Addictions, 19*(4), 419-430.

National Institute on Drug Abuse (NIDA). (1986). *A guide to mobilizing ethnic minority communities for drug abuse prevention.* Rockville, MD: NIDA.

Nowakowski, Jeri. (Ed.). (1986, March). The client perspective on evaluation. *New Directions for Program Evaluation, 36.*

Office for Substance Abuse Prevention (OSAP). (1989a, December). Collaborative evaluation. (Draft paper) *Cross-Site Evaluation.* Rockville, MD: OSAP.

Office for Substance Abuse Prevention (OSAP). (1989b). *Prevention Plus II: Tools for creating and sustaining drug-free communities.* Rockville, MD: OSAP.

Office for Substance Abuse Prevention (OSAP). (1990a, August). Accomplishments and lessons learned of high-risk youth grantees. (Draft paper) Cross-Site Evaluation. Rockville, MD: OSAP.

Office for Substance Abuse Prevention (OSAP). (1990b, August). Getting prevention to work: The OSAP experience 1986-1990. (Draft paper) Cross-Site Evaluation. Rockville, MD: OSAP.

Ogawa, Rodney T., & Malen, Betty. (1991, Fall). Towards rigor in reviews of multivocal literatures: Applying the exploratory case study method. Review of Educational Research, 61, 265-286.

Orlandi, Mario A. (1986, November). Community-based substance abuse prevention: A multicultural perspective. Journal of School Health, 56, 394-401.

Orlikowski, Wanda J., Baroudi, Jack J., & Rosen, Michael. (1988, August). Interpretivism as an alternative IS research paradigm. Paper presented at annual meeting of the Academy of Management, Anaheim, CA.

Patton, Michael Quinn. (1990). Qualitative evaluation and research methods, 2nd ed. Newbury Park, CA: Sage.

Pentz, Mary Ann, et al. (1986). Balancing program and research integrity in community drug abuse prevention: Project Star approach. Journal of School Health, 56(9), 389-393.

Perry, C. L., & Jessor, R. (1985). The concept of health promotion and the prevention of adolescent drug abuse. Health Education Quarterly, 12(2), 169-184.

Pyecha, John N., et al. (1988). A case study of the application of noncategorical special education in two states. Research Triangle Park, NC: Research Triangle Institute. (Robert K. Yin collaborated in the design, conduct, and analysis of the research.)

Room, Robin. (1987, Winter). Alcohol monopolies in the U.S.: Challenges and opportunities. Journal of Public Health Policy, 9, 509-530.

Room, Robin. (1990). Community action and alcohol problems: The demonstration project as an unstable mixture. In Norman Giesbrecht et al. (Eds.), Research, action, and the community: Experiences in the prevention of alcohol and other drug problems (pp. 1-25). Rockville, MD: Office for Substance Abuse Prevention.

Rossi, Peter H., & Freeman, Howard E. (1993). Evaluation: A systematic approach, 5th ed. Newbury Park, CA: Sage.

Rugg, Deborah L., et al. (1990). AIDS prevention evaluation: Conceptual and methodological issues. Evaluation and Program Planning, 13, 79-89.

Schaps, Eric, et al. (1982). Process and outcome evaluation of a drug education course. Journal of Drug Education, 12, 353-366.

Scheurich, James. (1990). A statewide evaluation system for school-based prevention programs and its research-suggesting results. In Ketty H. Rey et al. (Eds.), Prevention research findings, 1988 (pp. 54-92). Rockville, MD: Office for Substance Abuse Prevention.

Schinke, Steven P., et al. (1988). Preventing substance abuse among American-Indian adolescents: A bicultural competence skills approach. Journal of Counseling Psychology, 35, 87-90.

Schneider, Jane W., Griffith, Dan R., & Chasnoff, Ira J. (1989, July). Infants exposed to cocaine in utero: Implications for developmental assessment and intervention. Infants and Young Children, 2, 25-36.

Schuyler, Nancy Baenen, et al. (1985, June). Project Connect: 1984-85 final technical report. Austin, TX: Austin Independent School District.

Scriven, Michael. (1967). The methodology of evaluation. In Perspectives in curriculum evaluation. Chicago: Rand McNally.

Sidowski, J. B. (Ed.). (1966). *Experimental methods and instrumentation in psychology.* New York: McGraw-Hill.

Smith, John K., & Heshusius, Lous. (1986, January). Closing down the conversation: The end of the quantitative-qualitative debate among educational inquirers. *Educational Researcher,* 4-12.

Springer, J. Fred. (1990). Learning from prevention policy: A management focused approach. In Ketty H. Rey et al. (Eds.), *Prevention research findings, 1988* (pp. 231-242). Rockville, MD: Office for Substance Abuse Prevention.

Strauss, Anselm, & Corbin, Juliet. (1990). *Basics of qualitative research: Grounded theory procedures and techniques.* Newbury Park, CA: Sage.

Swisher, John D. (1990). What works? In Ketty H. Rey et al. (Eds.), *Prevention research findings, 1988* (pp. 14-23). Rockville, MD: Office for Substance Abuse Prevention.

Szanton, Peter. (1981). *Not well advised.* New York: Russell Sage.

Trochim, William M. K. (1989). Outcome pattern matching and program theory. *Evaluation and Program Planning, 1989, 12*(4), 355-366.

U.S. Department of Education in conjunction with U.S. Department of Health and Human Services. (1987, October). *Report to Congress and the White House on the nature and effectiveness of federal, state, and local drug prevention/education programs.* Washington, DC.

U.S. General Accounting Office. (1987, April/1991). *Case Study Evaluations.* Washington, DC: Program Evaluation and Methodology Division.

U.S. General Accounting Office. (1990, June). *Drug exposed infants: A generation at risk.* Washington, DC.

Van Maanen, John. (1988). *Tales from the field: On writing ethnography.* Chicago: University of Chicago Press.

Van Maanen, John, Dabbs, J. M., Jr., & Faulkner, R. R. (1982). *Varieties of qualitative research.* Newbury Park, CA: Sage.

White paper on drug abuse. (1975, September). A Report to the President from the Domestic Council Drug Abuse Task Force, Washington, DC.

Wholey, Joseph S. (1979). *Evaluation: Promise and performance.* Washington, DC: The Urban Institute.

Wittman, Friedner D. (1990). Environmental design to prevent problems of alcohol availability: Concepts and prospects. In Norman Giesbrecht et al. (Eds.), *Research, action, and the community: Experiences in the prevention of alcohol and other drug problems* (pp. 247-263). Rockville, MD: Office for Substance Abuse Prevention.

Yin, Robert K. (1981a, September). The case study as a serious research strategy. *Knowledge: Creation, Diffusion, Utilization, 3,* 97-114.

Yin, Robert K. (1981b, March). The case study crisis: Some answers. *Administrative Science Quarterly, 26,* 58-65.

Yin, Robert K. (1981c, January/February). Life histories of innovations: How new practices become routinized. *Public Administration Review, 41,* 21-28.

Yin, Robert K. (1982, September/October). Studying phenomenon and context across sites. *American Behavioral Scientist, 26,* 84-100.

Yin, Robert K. (1986). Community crime prevention: A synthesis of eleven evaluations. In Dennis P. Rosenbaum (Ed.), *Community crime prevention: Does it work?* (pp. 294-308). Beverly Hills, CA: Sage.

Yin, Robert K. (1984/1989). *Case study research: Design and methods.* Newbury Park, CA: Sage.

Yin, Robert K. (1991, Fall). Advancing rigorous methodologies: A review of "Towards rigor in reviews of multivocal literatures." *Review of Education Research, 61,* 299-305.

Yin, Robert K. (forthcoming). Evaluation: A singular craft. *New Directions in Program Evaluation.*

Yin, Robert K., Bateman, Peter G., & Moore, Gwendolyn B. (1985, March). Case studies and organizational innovation: Strengthening the connection. *Knowledge: Creation, Diffusion, Utilization, 6,* 249-260.

Yin, Robert K., & Gwaltney, Margaret K. (1981, June). Knowledge utilization as a networking process. *Knowledge: Creation, Diffusion, Utilization, 2,* 555-580.

Yin, Robert K., & Moore, Gwendolyn B. (1987). The use of advanced technologies in special education: Prospects from robotics, artificial intelligence, and computer simulation. *Journal of Learning Disabilities, 20*(1), 60-63.

Yin, Robert K., & Moore, Gwendolyn B. (1988, Fall). Lessons on the utilization of research from nine case experiences in the natural hazards field. *Knowledge in Society: The International Journal of Knowledge Transfer, 1,* 25-44.

Yin, Robert K., Schiller, Ellen P., & Teitelbaum, Michele. (1991, January). *Operation PAR (parental awareness and responsibility): A case study of a successful drug prevention and treatment program.* Washington, DC: National Prevention Evaluation Resource Network, COSMOS Corporation.

Yin, Robert K., Sottile, Stephanie A., & Bernstein, Nancy K. (1985, December). *Attracting high-technology firms to local areas: Lessons from nine high-technology and industrial parks.* Washington, DC: COSMOS Corporation.

Yin, Robert K., & White, J. Lynne. (1985). Microcomputer implementation in schools: Findings from twelve case studies. In Milton Chen & William Paisley (Eds.), *Children and microcomputers: Research on the newest medium* (pp. 109-128). Newbury Park, CA: Sage.

Yin, Robert K., & White, J. Lynne. (1986, September). *Managing for excellence in urban high schools: District and school roles.* Washington, DC: COSMOS Corporation.

Yin, Robert K., et al. (1979). *Changing urban bureaucracies: How new practices become routinized.* Lexington, MA: Lexington Books.

Yin, Robert K., et al. (1987, April). *Strengthening grass-roots, community organizations: An evaluation of a national program.* Washington, DC: COSMOS Corporation.

Yin, Robert K., et al. (1989, September). *Interorganizational partnerships in local job creation and job training efforts: Six case studies.* Washington, DC: COSMOS Corporation.

Author Index

Subject Index

About the Author

Robert K. Yin is President of COSMOS Corporation, a research and management technology firm specializing in social policy problems. Within the firm, he is involved with individual projects, including those using the case study method. Most of the applications reported in this book derive from work done with COSMOS's projects. He has authored numerous other books and articles. His first book on the case study method, *Case Study Research: Design and Methods,* has had two editions (1984, eight printings; 1989, thirteen printings) with a third now being prepared. He is a former member of the Rand Corporation (1970-1978) and a member of the Cosmos Club. He has also served as Visiting Scholar to the U.S. General Accounting Office during 1992-1993 (Program Evaluation and Methodology Division), and has served on the editorial boards of numerous journals, on peer review panels, and on committees of the National Academy of Sciences. He is known internationally for his presentations, seminars, and workshops on applied social research. A recent honor was his being invited to make a plenary presentation—"Evaluation: A Singular Craft"—at the American Evaluation Association (November 1992). He received his B.A. (magna cum laude) from Harvard College in 1962 (in History) and his Ph.D. in 1970 from the Department of Brain and Cognitive Sciences, Massachusetts Institute of Technology.